C000121319

Vegetarian Recipes

igloobooks

Published in 2016
by Igloo Books Ltd
Cottage Farm
Sywell
NN6 0BJ
www.igloobooks.com

Food photography and recipe development:
© Stockfood, The Food Media Agency
Cover image © Stockfood, The Food Media Agency

HUN001 0616
2 4 6 8 10 9 7 5 3
ISBN: 978-1-78557-534-1

Cover designed by Nicholas Gage
Interiors designed by Charles Wood-Penn
Edited by Natalie Baker

Printed and manufactured in China

Contents

Breakfasts

Croissants

MAKES **16**

PREPARATION TIME **2 HOURS + OVERNIGHT**

COOKING TIME **15 MINUTES**

INGREDIENTS

625 g / 1 lb 5 oz / 2 ¾ cups strong white (bread) flour

12 g / ½ oz salt

75 g / 3 oz / ⅓ cup sugar

20 g / ¾ oz dried yeast

500 g / 1 lb / 2 cups butter, cold, cubed

1 egg, beaten

METHOD

1. Place the flour, salt, sugar and yeast in a bowl and stir in enough water to make a pliable dough.

2. Tip the dough onto a floured surface, bring together and knead for 5–8 minutes, then refrigerate for 1 hour. Remove from the fridge and roll out on a floured surface into a 60 cm x 30 cm (24 in x 12 in) rectangle.

3. Roll out the butter into a 20 cm x 30 cm (8 in x 12 in) rectangle and place in the middle of the dough. Fold the remaining dough third over the butter layer so the dough now has three layers. Wrap in cling film and refrigerate for 1 hour.

4. Flour the work surface, then roll the dough out again to 60 cm x 30 cm (24 in x 12 in) and repeat the folding process. Refrigerate again for 1 hour. Repeat twice more, wrap in film and rest overnight.

5. The next day, roll out the dough to around 3 mm thickness and cut into 20 cm x 20 cm (8 in x 8 in) squares.

6. Cut each square in half diagonally to make 2 triangles and place on a lightly floured surface.

7. Roll each dough triangle up without pressing down too hard and curl round to make the traditional crescent shape. Place on lined baking trays and leave to rise for 1 hour in a warm place. Preheat the oven to 200°C (180°C fan) / 400F / gas 6.

8. Lightly brush with beaten egg and bake for about 15 minutes or until golden brown and crisp.

Chocolate Crêpes

SERVES 4

PREPARATION TIME 5 MINUTES

COOKING TIME 20 MINUTES

INGREDIENTS

150 g / 5 ½ oz / 1 cup plain (all-purpose) flour
1 large egg
325 ml / 11 ½ fl. oz / 1 ⅓ cup whole milk
30 g / 1 oz butter, melted
1 tsp cocoa powder
1 orange, segmented and cubed
a few sprigs mint

For the filling
100 ml / 3 ½ fl. oz / ½ cup double
    (heavy) cream
100 g / 3 ½ oz / ¾ cup dark chocolate (minimum
    60 % cocoa solids), chopped to serve

METHOD

1. To make the filling, heat the cream to simmering point, then pour it over the chocolate and stir to emulsify. Leave to cool and thicken slightly while you make the crêpes.

2. Sieve the flour into a bowl and make a well in the centre. Break in the egg and pour in the milk, then use a whisk to gradually incorporate all of the flour from round the outside.

3. Melt the butter in a small frying pan, then whisk it into the batter.

4. Put the buttered frying pan back over a low heat. Add a small ladle of batter and swirl the pan to coat the bottom.

5. When it starts to dry and curl up at the edges, turn the pancake over with a spatula and cook the other side until golden brown and cooked through.

6. Repeat with the rest of the mixture, then serve each crêpe rolled up with a big spoonful of chocolate filling inside.

7. Sprinkle over a little cocoa powder and arrange some orange and mint on the side.

TOP TIP
Stir 2 chopped bananas into the chocolate filling and omit the garnish.

Stuffed Tomatoes

SERVES 4

PREPARATION TIME **10 MINUTES**

COOKING TIME **10–15 MINUTES**

INGREDIENTS

40 g / 1 oz / ¼ cup butter
6 eggs, lightly beaten
6 tsp double (heavy) cream
1 tbsp parsley, chopped
4 large tomatoes
salt and freshly ground black pepper

METHOD

1. Preheat the oven to 200°C (180°C fan) / 400F / gas 7.

2. Heat most of the butter in a pan until foaming, then stir in the eggs.

3. Cook gently, stirring thoroughly with a wooden spoon until lightly cooked with some liquid egg still left.

4. Stir in the cream and parsley, then season with salt and pepper.

5. Core the tomatoes and scoop a little of the flesh from inside, then spoon the egg into the cavity.

6. Place in a roasting tin and cook for around 10–15 minutes or until the tomatoes have softened, then serve.

TOP TIP
Add 6 button mushrooms, finely chopped, to the pan before the eggs.

Mixed Pepper Tortilla

SERVES 6

PREPARATION TIME 30 MINUTES

COOKING TIME 35 MINUTES

INGREDIENTS

1 red pepper, deseeded and cut in half
1 yellow pepper, deseeded and cut in half
4 tbsp olive oil
8 eggs
1 tbsp crème fraiche
1 clove garlic, crushed
½ bunch parsley, chopped
salt and freshly ground black pepper

METHOD

1. Preheat the oven to 200°C (180°C fan) / 400F / gas 7.

2. Place the pepper halves in a roasting tin, drizzle with oil and roast for about 30 minutes or until soft and blackened.

3. Remove from the tin, place in a freezer bag and leave to steam.

4. Once cooled, remove the skins from the peppers and roughly chop the flesh.

5. Beat the eggs with the crème fraiche in a large bowl.

6. Add the peppers, garlic and parsley, then season and mix together carefully.

7. Oil a large frying pan, then pour the mixture in and bake at 180°C / 350F for about 35 minutes until puffed and golden. The egg should be cooked through.

8. Cut into squares and serve warm or cold.

TOP TIP
Serve with a dollop of crème fraiche sprinkled with smoked paprika.

Tomato, Coriander and Feta Tortilla

SERVES 4

PREPARATION TIME 30 MINUTES

COOKING TIME 30 MINUTES

INGREDIENTS

6 eggs
1 tbsp crème fraiche
8 cherry tomatoes, halved
100 g / 3 ½ fl. oz / ½ cup feta cheese, cubed
6 sprigs coriander (cilantro), chopped
olive oil
salt and freshly ground black pepper

METHOD

1. Preheat the oven to 180°C (160°C fan) / 350F / gas 5.

2. Beat the eggs with the crème fraiche in a large bowl.

3. Add tomatoes, feta, coriander and seasoning, then mix together carefully.

4. Oil a large frying pan, then pour the mixture in and bake for about 35 minutes until puffed and golden. The egg should be cooked through.

5. Cut into squares and serve warm or cold.

TOP TIP

Try goats' cheese instead of feta and swap the coriander with parsley.

Courgette, Tomato and Feta Frittata

SERVES 6

PREPARATION TIME 30 MINUTES

COOKING TIME 35 MINUTES

INGREDIENTS

8 eggs
1 tbsp crème fraiche
2 courgettes (zucchinis), finely diced
handful sun-dried tomatoes, finely chopped
100 g / 3 ½ fl. oz / ½ cup feta cheese, cubed
6 sprigs thyme
olive oil
salt and freshly ground black pepper

METHOD

1. Preheat the oven to 180°C (160°C fan) / 350F / gas 5.

2. Beat the eggs with the crème fraiche in a large bowl.

3. Add the courgettes, tomatoes, feta and thyme leaves, then season and mix together carefully.

4. Oil a large frying pan, then pour the mixture in and bake for about 35 minutes until puffed and golden. The egg should be cooked through.

5. Cut into squares and serve warm or cold.

TOP TIP

Substitute the feta with taleggio cheese for an oozing frittata.

Green Asparagus Frittata

SERVES 6

PREPARATION TIME 30 MINUTES

COOKING TIME 35 MINUTES

INGREDIENTS

8 eggs
1 tbsp crème fraiche
1 bunch asparagus
1 onion, peeled and thickly sliced
olive oil
salt and freshly ground black pepper

METHOD

1. Preheat the oven to 180°C (160°C fan) / 350F / gas 5.

2. Beat the eggs with the crème fraiche in a large bowl.

3. Snap the woody ends off the asparagus and discard. Cut the asparagus into short lengths.

4. Fry the onion gently in 2 tbsp olive oil until deep gold and soft; about 20 minutes.

5. Pour the egg mixture in, add the asparagus and distribute evenly. Season with salt and pepper.

6. Bake for about 35 minutes until puffed and golden. The egg should be cooked through.

7. Cut into squares and serve warm or cold.

TOP TIP

Serve alongside some wilted spinach and garlic with a squeeze of lemon juice.

Onion and Mint Omelette

SERVES 4

PREPARATION TIME 5 MINUTES

COOKING TIME 8 MINUTES

INGREDIENTS

1 tbsp olive oil
1 tbsp butter
1 onion, very finely sliced
4 eggs
½ bunch mint leaves, finely chopped
salt and freshly ground black pepper

METHOD

1. Heat the oil and butter in a large frying pan and cook the onions slowly until golden and sweet.

2. Meanwhile crack the eggs into a bowl and beat lightly. Tip into the pan and swirl gently to cover the base of the pan and help it set.

3. When the omelette is nearly set, sprinkle over the mint and seasoning and flash under a hot grill to set it completely.

4. Remove from the pan and serve.

TOP TIP
Use parsley instead of mint and add 1 finely chopped clove of garlic to the egg mix.

Sultana Brioche

SERVES 8

PREPARATION TIME 4 MINUTES

COOKING TIME 30 MINUTES

INGREDIENTS

125 ml / 4 fl. oz / ½ cup milk

1 egg

160 g / 5 oz / ⅔ cup plain (all-purpose) flour

160 g / 5 oz / ⅔ cup strong white bread flour

1 tsp salt

1 ½ tbsp sugar

1 x 7 g sachet easy-blend dried yeast

200 g / 7 oz / ¾ cup unsalted butter, chilled and cubed

4–5 tbsp sultanas

METHOD

1. Lightly grease a 23 cm x 13 cm (9 in x 5 in) loaf tin. Warm the milk with 3 tbsp water, add the egg and whisk.

2. Place the flours, salt, sugar and yeast in a food processor and mix, then add the butter a little at a time and pulse to cut the butter into the flour. Don't let it become breadcrumbs.

3. Tip the flour-butter mixture into a bowl, make a well in the centre and add the milk mixture and sultanas, then fold together with a fork. It does not need to be completely smooth.

4. Pour into the loaf tin, cover with cling film and leave to prove in a warm draught-free place for 1 hour. Preheat the oven to 200°C (180°C fan) / 400F / gas 7.

5. Remove the cling film and bake for about 30 minutes or until risen and golden. Leave to cool before eating.

TOP TIP

Slice and serve with jam (jelly) or chocolate spread for a sweet breakfast.

25

Hard-boiled Eggs with Béchamel Sauce

SERVES 4

PREPARATION TIME 20 MINUTES

COOKING TIME 15 MINUTES

INGREDIENTS

4 eggs
1 tbsp butter
1 tbsp plain (all-purpose) flour
300 ml / 10 fl. oz / 1 ¼ cups milk
1 bay leaf
salt and freshly ground black pepper

METHOD

1. Place the eggs in cold water, bring to a simmer and cook for 6 minutes.

2. Place in cold water to stop the cooking, then peel carefully.

3. To make the sauce, melt the butter in a pan, then stir in the flour to make a paste.

4. Whisk in the milk a little at a time, stirring until the sauce is smooth and thick. Add the bay leaf and leave to cook for 10 minutes, stirring occasionally. Season to taste.

5. Cut the eggs in half and place in a dish. Spoon over the béchamel and grill until golden and bubbling.

TOP TIP

Serve with fresh, warm granary bread for a hearty breakfast.

Baked Eggs with Mushrooms

SERVES 4

PREPARATION TIME 10 MINUTES

COOKING TIME 15 MINUTES

INGREDIENTS

100 g / 3 ½ oz / ½ cup mushrooms, finely sliced
60 g / 2 oz / ¼ cup butter
4 eggs
salt and freshly ground black pepper

METHOD

1. Preheat the oven to 190°C (170°C fan) / 375F / gas 5.

2. Cook the mushrooms in foaming butter in a pan until turning golden.

3. Butter 4 ramekin dishes generously and crack the eggs into the ramekins.

4. Spoon the mushrooms around and top with a little butter and seasoning.

5. Place the ramekins in a roasting tin, pour in enough boiling water to come halfway up the sides of the ramekins and bake in the oven for 15 minutes or until the eggs are just set.

TOP TIP
Serve with a scattering of chopped tarragon before serving for a herbal twist.

Baked Egg with Garlic and Tomato

SERVES 4

PREPARATION TIME 10 MINUTES

COOKING TIME 15–20 MINUTES

INGREDIENTS

60 g / 2 oz / ¼ cup butter
2 tomatoes, halved
1 clove garlic, crushed
4 eggs
salt and freshly ground black pepper

METHOD

1. Preheat the oven to 190°C (170°C fan) / 375F / gas 5.

2. Butter 4 ramekin dishes generously and place a tomato half in the bottom, topped with a little garlic and salt and pepper.

3. Crack the eggs into the ramekins on top of the tomato and dot with butter.

4. Place the ramekins in a roasting tin, pour in enough boiling water to come halfway up the sides of the ramekins and bake in the oven for 15–20 minutes or until the eggs are just set.

TOP TIP

Add ½ finely chopped red chilli (chili) over the tomato before the egg for a kick.

Eggs Florentine with Mornay Sauce

SERVES 4

PREPARATION TIME 5 MINUTES

COOKING TIME 8 MINUTES

INGREDIENTS

4 eggs
2 handfuls spinach leaves
1 tbsp butter
4 slices bread, toasted
salt and freshly ground black pepper

For the Mornay sauce
150 ml / 5 fl. oz / ²/₃ cup milk
150 ml / 5 fl. oz / ²/₃ cup single cream
1 tsp Dijon mustard
1 tbsp plain (all-purpose) flour
½ tbsp butter
50 g / 1 ¾ oz / ¼ cup Cheddar, grated
1 tbsp vegetarian Parmesan, grated
½ bunch parsley, chopped

METHOD

1. To make the Mornay sauce, whisk the milk, cream, mustard, flour and butter in a pan over medium heat until smooth and thick.

2. Whisk in the cheeses and stir to melt, then cook the sauce over a low heat for 5 minutes to cook out the flour.

3. Add the parsley, season well, set aside and keep warm.

4. Poach the eggs in boiling water for about 3 minutes for a runny yolk. Remove to kitchen paper and leave to drain.

5. Wilt the spinach in a pan, then squeeze out any excess moisture and stir in the butter to melt.

6. Toast the bread and top with the spinach. Place an egg on top, then spoon over the Mornay sauce and season to taste.

TOP TIP
Squeeze over some lemon juice for a little extra zing.

Hazelnut and Walnut Bread

SERVES 4

PREPARATION TIME 2 HOURS

COOKING TIME 25 MINUTES

INGREDIENTS

475 g / 16 oz / 2 cup malthouse flour
1 tbsp soft brown sugar
1 ½ tsp salt
1 ½ tsp fast-action dried yeast
2 tbsp vegetable oil
325 ml / 11 fl. oz / 1 ⅓ cup warm water
200 g / 7 oz / 3 ½ cup mixed hazelnuts (cobnuts)
    and walnuts, chopped

METHOD

1. Mix the flour, sugar, salt and yeast in a bowl, add the oil and stir in enough water to make a smooth dough.

2. Knead on a floured surface for 5 minutes until smooth and elastic. Work in the walnuts and hazelnuts, then return to the bowl. Cover loosely and leave in a warm place to rise for 1 hour or until doubled in size.

3. Tip onto a floured surface, knead well for 5 minutes then shape into an oval loaf.

4. Transfer to a greased baking sheet and make deep slashes in the top. Cover loosely and leave to rise for 30 minutes or until half as big again.

5. Preheat the oven to 200°C (180°C fan) / 400F / gas 6.

6. Sprinkle with a little extra flour, lightly spray with water and bake for 25 minutes or until browned and the bread sounds hollow when tapped. Transfer to a wire rack to cool.

TOP TIP
Add a handful of sultanas to the mix for a fruity burst.

Scrambled Eggs and Mushrooms on Toast

SERVES 4

PREPARATION TIME 5 MINUTES

COOKING TIME 10 MINUTES

INGREDIENTS

60 g / 1 oz / ¼ cup butter
70 g / 2 ½ oz / ⅓ cup button mushrooms, halved
6 eggs
4 tsp double (heavy) cream
1 tbsp parsley, chopped
4 thick slices bread, toasted and buttered
salt and freshly ground black pepper

METHOD

1. Heat the butter in a pan and cook the mushrooms until golden and all the excess moisture has evaporated.

2. Crack the eggs into a bowl and beat lightly.

3. Stir the eggs into the pan and cook gently, stirring thoroughly with a wooden spoon until lightly cooked with some liquid egg still left.

4. Stir in the cream and parsley, then season well. Serve immediately with the toast.

TOP TIP
Sourdough bread works well here. Try rubbing on a little garlic before the butter.

Toasted Muffin with Scrambled Egg

SERVES **4**

PREPARATION TIME **5 MINUTES**

COOKING TIME **8 MINUTES**

INGREDIENTS

6 eggs
4 English muffins, split horizontally
40 g / 1 oz / ¼ cup butter
6 tsp double (heavy) cream
salt and freshly ground black pepper

METHOD

1. Crack the eggs into a bowl and beat lightly.

2. Heat most of the butter in a pan until foaming, then stir in the eggs.

3. Cook gently, stirring thoroughly with a wooden spoon until lightly cooked with some liquid egg still left.

4. Stir in the cream and season, then serve immediately with the toasted muffins.

TOP TIP

Stir in ½ bunch chopped chives or chervil with the cream.

Fig and Orange Muffins

MAKES **12**

PREPARATION TIME **25 MINUTES**

COOKING TIME **20–25 MINUTES**

INGREDIENTS

1 large egg
120 ml / 4 fl. oz / ½ cup sunflower oil
120 ml / 4 fl. oz / ½ cup milk
375 g / 12 ½ oz / 2 ½ cups self-raising flour, sifted
1 tsp baking powder
200 g / 7 oz / ¾ cup caster (superfine) sugar
1 orange, zest finely grated
4 fresh figs, chopped

METHOD

1. Preheat the oven to 180°C (160°C fan) / 350F / gas 4 and line a 12-hole muffin tin with greaseproof paper.

2. Beat the egg in a jug with the oil and milk until well mixed.

3. Mix the flour, baking powder, sugar and orange zest in a bowl.

4. Pour in the egg mixture and stir just enough to combine, then fold through the figs.

5. Divide the mixture between the paper cases and bake for 20–25 minutes.

6. Test with a wooden toothpick, if it comes out clean, the cakes are done.

7. Transfer the muffins to a wire rack and leave to cool completely.

TOP TIP

For a sharper tasting muffin use the zest of two lemons instead of the oranges.

Poached Egg with Mushrooms

SERVES **4**

PREPARATION TIME **5 MINUTES**

COOKING TIME **10 MINUTES**

INGREDIENTS

60 g / 2 oz / ¼ cup butter
100 g / 3 ½ oz / ½ cup mixed wild mushrooms
4 eggs
salt and freshly ground black pepper

METHOD

1. Heat the butter in a pan until foaming, then add the mushrooms.

2. Cook until tender and any excess moisture has evaporated. Season and keep warm.

3. Poach the eggs in boiling water for about 3 minutes for a runny yolk. Remove to kitchen paper and leave to drain.

4. Serve the egg on a bed of mushrooms.

TOP TIP
Serve with grilled vine tomatoes and toast for a substantial breakfast.

Cinnamon Buns

MAKES 24

PREPARATION TIME 2 HOURS

COOKING TIME 30 MINUTES

INGREDIENTS

75 ml / 3 fl. oz / 1/3 cup lukewarm water
1/2 tsp dried yeast
50 ml / 1 3/4 fl. oz / 1/4 cup maple syrup
50 ml / 1 3/4 fl. oz / 1/4 cup butter, melted
1 egg, beaten
1/2 tsp salt
500 g / 1 lb / 2 cups plain (all-purpose) flour

For the filling

40 g / 1 1/2 oz butter, melted
1 tbsp ground cinnamon
1/4 tsp grated nutmeg
2 tbsp soft dark brown sugar
2 tbsp maple syrup
3 tbsp pecans, chopped
2 tbsp sultanas

METHOD

1. Tip the water, yeast and half of the maple syrup into a bowl and leave for 15 minutes until it starts to bubble.

2. Add the remaining syrup, melted butter, egg and salt and mix well. Tip the flour into a bowl and make a well in the centre. Pour in the yeast mixture and bring the flour into the liquid until everything is combined.

3. Tip out of the bowl onto a floured surface and knead for 8–10 minutes. Place back into the bowl, cover and leave to rise for 1 hour.

4. Preheat the oven to 170°C (150°C fan) / 325F / gas 4.

5. Knock the dough back and roll on a floured surface to make a 38 cm x 25 cm (15 in x 10 in) rectangle. Brush with melted butter, then sprinkle over the filling ingredients.

6. Roll the dough up like a sausage. Stretch it out with your hands to about 60 cm (24 in) in length, then cut into 5–6 cm (2–2 1/2 in) lengths and place in greased muffin tins. Bake in the oven for 30 minutes, then remove to a wire rack to cool.

TOP TIP

Use dried cranberries in place of the sultanas.

45

French Toast

METHOD

1. Whisk together the eggs, milk, vanilla and cinnamon, then pour into a bowl.

2. Lay the bread in the mixture, soaking it thoroughly for a few minutes.

3. Heat the oil in a pan and gently fry the bread slices until golden and crisp on each side. Serve hot.

SERVES 4

PREPARATION TIME 15 MINUTES

COOKING TIME 10 MINUTES

INGREDIENTS

2 eggs, beaten
300 ml / 10 fl. oz / 1 ¼ cups full-fat milk or single (half-and-half) cream
1 tsp vanilla extract
½ tsp ground cinnamon
4 thick slices white bread
2 tbsp vegetable oil

TOP TIP

Omit the vanilla extract and add some finely chopped chives to the mixture.

Soups and Salads

Feta and Cherry Tomato Salad

METHOD

1. Arrange the lettuce leaves on two plates and top with the feta, tomatoes and olives.

2. Drizzle with olive oil and sprinkle with pink peppercorns.

ERVES 2

REPARATION TIME 5 MINUTES

NGREDIENTS

large lettuce leaves
)0 g / 3 ½ oz / ²/₃ cup feta, cubed
cherry tomatoes, quartered
few Kalamata olives
tbsp extra virgin olive oil
tsp pink peppercorns, crushed

TOP TIP

Cut half a cucumber into cubes and toss with the feta, olives and tomatoes.

Vegetable Soup

SERVES 4–6

PREPARATION TIME 15 MINUTES

COOKING TIME 20–25 MINUTES

INGREDIENTS

3 tbsp olive oil
1 large onion, chopped
2 carrots, roughly chopped
2 sticks celery, chopped
2 large potatoes, peeled and chopped
1 clove garlic, finely chopped
2 bay leaves
2 x 400 g can chopped tomatoes
1.5 litres / 3 pints / 6 ⅓ cups vegetable stock
large handful green beans, chopped
50 g / 1 ¾ oz / ¼ cup peas
extra virgin olive oil
vegetarian Parmesan, to serve
salt and freshly ground black pepper

METHOD

1. Heat the oil in a large pan and sweat the onion, carrot and celery until beginning to soften.

2. Add the potatoes, garlic and bay leaves and cook for 3 minutes, then add the tomatoes and stock and bring to a simmer.

3. Cook for 10 minutes, then add the beans and peas and leave to simmer for another 6–7 minutes until all is tender.

4. Season well, then serve warm with a drizzle of extra virgin olive oil and a generous grating of vegetarian Parmesan and seasoning.

TOP TIP
Serve with warm, rustic bread, thickly sliced.

Waldorf Salad

METHOD

1. Place the celery, walnuts, grapes and apple in a bowl.

2. Mix together the mayonnaise, a little lemon juice and seasoning.

3. Stir into the salad ingredients and serve on the lettuce leaves.

SERVES 4

PREPARATION TIME 15 MINUTES

INGREDIENTS

225 g / 8 oz / 1 cup celery sticks, finely chopped
225 g / 8 oz / 1 cup walnuts, toasted under a
    hot grill
225 g / 8 oz / 1 cup seedless grapes, halved
2 eating apples, cored and thinly sliced
6 tbsp mayonnaise
½ lemon, juiced
lettuce leaves, to serve
salt and freshly ground black pepper

TOP TIP
Stir a handful of finely chopped parsley or tarragon into the mayonnaise.

Creamy Tomato Soup

SERVES **4**

PREPARATION TIME **10 MINUTES**

COOKING TIME **30 MINUTES**

INGREDIENTS

400 g / 14 oz / 2 ½ cup tomatoes
2 tbsp olive oil
1 onion, finely chopped
2 cloves garlic, crushed
1 tbsp tomato purée
1 litre / 1 pint 15 fl. oz / 4 cups vegetable stock
2 tbsp crème fraiche
2 tbsp flat-leaf parsley, chopped
salt and freshly ground black pepper

METHOD

1. Score a cross in the top of the tomatoes and blanch them in boiling water for 30 seconds

2. Plunge them into cold water, then peel off the skins.

3. Cut the tomatoes in half and remove the seeds, then cut the flesh into small cubes.

4. Heat the oil in a saucepan and fry the onion for 5 minutes or until softened. Add the garlic and cook for 2 more minutes, then stir in the tomatoes and tomato purée.

5. Pour in the vegetable stock and bring to the boil.

6. Simmer for 20 minutes, then stir in the crème fraiche and blend until smooth with a stick blender.

7. Try the soup and adjust the seasoning with salt and pepper.

8. Stir in the parsley, then ladle into warm bowls

TOP TIP
Replace the parsley with a small bunch of roughly chopped basil.

Asparagus and Parmesan Salad

SERVES 4

PREPARATION TIME 5 MINUTES

COOKING TIME 6 MINUTES

INGREDIENTS

200 g / 7 oz / 2 cups / 1 cup asparagus, trimmed
100 g / 3 ½ oz / ²⁄₃ cup cherry tomatoes,
    quartered
3 baby spring onions (scallions), halved
    lengthways
75 g / 2 ½ oz / ½ cup Kalamata olives
2 tbsp sesame seeds
30 g / 1 oz / ¼ cup vegetarian Parmesan
100 g / 3 ½ oz / 2 cups mixed salad leaves
a few sprigs flowering thyme to garnish

For the dressing

1 tbsp mayonnaise
1 tbsp natural yogurt
1 tbsp lemon juice
1 tsp fresh thyme leaves, chopped

METHOD

1. Blanch the asparagus in boiling, salted water for 6 minutes or until al dente. Plunge into cold water and drain well.

2. Divide the leaves between four plates and top with the asparagus, tomatoes, spring onions and olives.

3. Sprinkle over the sesame seeds and use a vegetable peeler to shave over some Parmesan.

4. Mix the dressing ingredients together and drizzle over the salad, then garnish with flowering thyme.

TOP TIP
Add some toasted pumpkin seeds for a delicious crunch.

Cream of Asparagus Soup

SERVES 4

PREPARATION TIME 5 MINUTES

COOKING TIME 25–30 MINUTES

INGREDIENTS

450 g / 1 lb / 2 cups asparagus, woody ends
    trimmed off and reserved, the rest chopped
1 litre / 2 ¼ pints / 4 ¼ cups vegetable stock
30 g / 1 oz butter
1 potato, peeled and chopped
100 ml / 3 ½ fl. oz / ½ cup single
    (half-and-half) cream
1 tbsp parsley, chopped
salt and freshly ground black pepper

METHOD

1. Add the asparagus ends to the stock and bring to the boil, simmering for about 15 minutes, then strain.

2. Heat the butter in a pan, add the remaining asparagus and potato and cook for five minutes.

3. Stir in the strained stock, bring to the boil and simmer for five to ten minutes until the vegetables are tender.

4. Blend using a stick blender, then return to the pan.

5. Add the single cream and reheat gently without boiling. Season and stir through the parsley before serving.

TOP TIP
Purée a small bag of watercress with the ingredients.

Broccoli, Tomato and Coriander Salad

ERVES 4

REPARATION TIME 5 MINUTES

OOKING TIME 10–12 MINUTES

NGREDIENTS

small head broccoli, broken into small florets
tsp coriander seeds
tomatoes, cut into wedges
small bunch fresh coriander (cilantro),
   leaves only
 lemon, juiced
tbsp extra virgin olive oil
alt and freshly ground black pepper

METHOD

1. Blanch the broccoli in boiling, salted water for 3–4 minutes or until just tender. Drain well.

2. Meanwhile, dry fry the coriander seeds until fragrant, shaking the pan regularly.

3. Toss the drained broccoli with the tomatoes and coriander leaves and split between 4 serving plates.

4. Sprinkle over the coriander seeds and dress with the lemon juice and olive oil.

5. Season with salt and pepper just before serving.

TOP TIP

Substitute the broccoli with cauliflower florets and proceed as above.

63

Tomato, Pepper and Bean Soup

SERVES 4

PREPARATION TIME 15 MINUTES

COOKING TIME 20 MINUTES

INGREDIENTS

4 tbsp olive oil
1 onion, peeled and finely sliced
2 cloves garlic, finely sliced
2 red peppers, deseeded and finely sliced
2 yellow peppers, deseeded and finely sliced
1 tbsp tomato purée
2 x 400 g can chopped tomatoes
750 ml / 1 ⅓ pints / 3 cups vegetable stock
2 x 400 g can cannellini beans, drained
1 sprig rosemary
2 sprigs thyme
1 bay leaf
extra virgin olive oil
salt and freshly ground black pepper

METHOD

1. Heat the oil in a pan and cook the onion until golden.

2. Add the garlic and peppers and cook until softened.

3. Stir through the tomato purée and cook out for 2 minutes, then add the tomatoes, stock and beans.

4. Throw in the herbs, bring to a simmer and cook for at least 20 minutes until rich and slightly thickened.

5. If desired, crush the beans slightly with a potato masher to thicken the soup. Season well.

6. Serve in deep bowls drizzled with extra virgin olive oil.

TOP TIP
Sprinkle over some vegetarian Parmesan for a cheesy topping.

Watermelon, Feta and Basil Salad

ERVES 4

REPARATION TIME 5 MINUTES

NGREDIENTS

small watermelon, deseeded and cut into
    chunks
00 g / 3 ½ oz / ⅔ cup feta, cubed
tbsp basil leaves, shredded
tbsp extra virgin olive oil

METHOD

1. Mix the watermelon with the feta and divide between four plates.

2. Scatter over the basil and drizzle with olive oil, then sprinkle with sea salt.

TOP TIP

Replace the basil with fresh mint leaves and a squeeze of lemon juice.

Leek and Potato Soup

SERVES **4**

PREPARATION TIME **10 MINUTES**

COOKING TIME **20–25 MINUTES**

INGREDIENTS

60 g / 2 oz / ¼ cup butter
4 leeks, green ends discarded and finely sliced
2 floury potatoes, peeled and diced
2 sprigs thyme
850 ml / 1 ½ pints / 3 ½ cups chicken or
    vegetable stock
250 ml / 9 fl. oz / 1 cup milk
½ bunch chives, chopped
salt and white pepper

METHOD

1. In a large pan melt the butter until it starts to foam, then add the leeks. Cook gently over a low heat until soft.

2. Add the potatoes and thyme and cook for a couple of minutes. Add the stock and milk, bring to a simmer and cook gently for 20–25 minutes, until the potatoes are soft.

3. Remove the thyme stalks and blend with a stick blender until smooth.

4. Return to the heat and reheat, seasoning carefully. Serve with chives sprinkled on top.

TOP TIP
Serve very chilled for a refreshing summer starter.

Rice Salad with Orange and Figs

ERVES 4

REPARATION TIME 5 MINUTES

OOKING TIME 20 MINUTES

NGREDIENTS

00 g / 7 oz / 1 ¼ cup long-grain rice
cucumber, sliced
orange, peeled and sliced
dried figs, chopped
dried apricots, sliced
tbsp pistachios, chopped
tbsp chives, chopped

or the dressing
tsp runny honey
lemon, juiced
tbsp olive oil

METHOD

1. Put the rice in a saucepan and add enough water to cover it by 1 cm (½ in).

2. Bring the pan to the boil, then cover and reduce the heat to a low setting.

3. Cook for 10 minutes, then turn off the heat and leave to stand for 10 minutes without lifting the lid.

4. Whisk the honey with the lemon juice, then whisk in the olive oil.

5. When the rice is ready, combine it with the rest of the ingredients and dressing and season well with salt and pepper.

6. Serve warm or at room temperature.

TOP TIP

Replace the orange with grapefruit segments and the figs with chopped, stoned dates.

Indian Tomato and Lentil Soup

SERVES 4

PREPARATION TIME 15 MINUTES

COOKING TIME 35–40 MINUTES

INGREDIENTS

50 ml / 1 ½ fl. oz / ¼ cup olive oil
1 large onion, finely chopped
2 cloves garlic, minced
3.5 cm (1 in) piece of ginger, minced
1 tbsp ground coriander
2 tsp ground cumin
1 tsp Madras curry powder
½ tsp chilli (chili) powder
½ tsp turmeric
250 g / 9 oz / 1 cup split lentils
4 large tomatoes, roughly chopped
1.4 litres / 2 ½ pints / 5 cups vegetable stock
coriander (cilantro) leaves, to garnish
salt and freshly ground black pepper

METHOD

1. Heat the olive oil in a large saucepan set over a medium heat. Sweat the onion, garlic and ginger for 6–8 minutes until soft and starting to brown.

2. Add the spices and some salt and pepper. Stir well and cook for a few minutes over a reduced heat.

3. Add the lentils and tomatoes, stir well, then cover with the stock. Bring to the boil, skimming any scum that comes to the surface.

4. Boil for 5 minutes, then reduce to a simmer and cook for 20–25 minutes until the lentils have absorbed half of the stock.

5. Remove from the heat and purée roughly using a stick blender.

6. Return to the heat and adjust the seasoning to taste. Ladle into serving bowls and garnish with coriander before serving.

TOP TIP

Serve with a dollop of plain yogurt for a cooling sauce.

Couscous Salad

SERVES 4

PREPARATION TIME 5 MINUTES

COOKING TIME 5 MINUTES

INGREDIENTS

300 g / 10 ½ oz / 1 ¾ cup couscous
1 red pepper, cubed
1 green pepper, cubed
1 tomato, deseeded and cubed
1 tbsp mint, chopped

For the dressing
1 tsp runny honey
1 lemon, juiced
1 tbsp olive oil

METHOD

1. Put the couscous in a large serving bowl and pour over 300 ml / 10 fl. oz / 1 ¼ cups of boiling water.

2. Cover the bowl with cling film and let it stand for 5 minutes, then fluff up the grains with a fork.

3. Stir through the peppers, tomato and mint.

4. Whisk the honey with the lemon juice, then whisk in the olive oil.

5. Pour the dressing over the couscous and serve.

TOP TIP
Add a little chopped chilli (chili) for extra kick.

Minestrone Soup

SERVES 4

PREPARATION TIME 20 MINUTES

COOKING TIME 60–90 MINUTES

INGREDIENTS

2 tbsp olive oil
1 onion, peeled and finely chopped
2 celery stalks, finely chopped
2 carrots, peeled and finely chopped
2 cloves of garlic, finely chopped
2 potatoes, peeled and finely chopped
2 tomatoes, peeled and finely chopped
1.5 litres / 2 ½ pints / 5 ½ cups vegetable stock
200 g / 6 ½ oz / ¾ cup greens, finely sliced
100 g / 3 ½ oz / ½ cup macaroni pasta
salt and pepper
vegetarian Parmesan
extra virgin olive oil

METHOD

1. Heat the oil in a large pan and gently fry the vegetables in the order listed. Stir regularly and give each one a good 5 minutes to cook without colouring before adding the next one.

2. Pour in the stock and bring to a gentle simmer, then cook very gently for about an hour.

3. Add the greens and the pasta and cook for a further 30 minutes.

4. Adjust the seasoning.

5. Serve warm, sprinkled with Parmesan and drizzled with olive oil.

TOP TIP

If you don't have macaroni to hand, broken strands of spaghetti work just as well.

Greek Salad

METHOD

1. Halve the cherry tomatoes and place in a bowl with a little salt and a drizzle of olive oil. Leave for up to 30 minutes.

2. Halve the cucumber lengthways, then scrape out the seeds with a teaspoon. Slice the halves into half-moons, then place in a colander, sprinkle with a little salt and leave to drain for 30 minutes.

3. When the tomatoes and cucumber are ready, combine them in a large salad bowl with the red onion and olives and crumble in the feta cheese.

4. In a separate bowl, whisk together the vinegar, a little seasoning and the oregano, then whisk in enough extra virgin olive oil to make a thickened dressing.

5. Drizzle the dressing over the salad vegetables and toss thoroughly before serving.

SERVES 4

PREPARATION TIME 40 MINUTES

INGREDIENTS

0 g / 5 oz / ⅔ cup cherry tomatoes

tsp olive oil

cucumber

red onion, halved and finely sliced

0 g / 5 oz / ⅔ cup black olives, stoned

0 g / 7 oz / ¾ cup feta cheese

3 tbsp red wine vinegar

sp dried oregano or small handful fresh oregano leaves

8 tbsp extra virgin olive oil

lt and freshly ground black pepper

TOP TIP

Try basil-infused olive oil for a twist on this classic salad.

Parmesan Soup

SERVES 4

PREPARATION TIME 5 MINUTES

COOKING TIME 15 MINUTES

INGREDIENTS

1.5 litres / 2 pints 12 fl. oz / 6 cups vegetable
    stock
2 eggs
2 tbsp vegetarian Parmesan, grated
bunch basil leaves
250 g / 9 oz / 2 cups spinach leaves, shredded
nutmeg
salt and pepper

METHOD

1. Bring the vegetable stock to the boil in a pan.

2. Whisk together the eggs, Parmesan and basil until completely blended.

3. Lower the heat. Whisking constantly in a figure of eight motion, stir the egg mixture into the stock a little at a time until all is incorporated.

4. Leave to simmer very gently for about 5 minutes until thickened.

5. Stir through the spinach and a little grated nutmeg.

6. Adjust the seasoning before serving.

TOP TIP

This soup is delicious served with warm focaccia.

Sweetcorn and Pepper Salad

SERVES 4

PREPARATION TIME 5 MINUTES

INGREDIENTS

iceberg lettuce leaves
400 g / 14 oz / 4 cups canned sweetcorn, drained
red pepper, cubed
green pepper, cubed
cucumber, cubed
hard-boiled eggs, halved
tomato, quartered
black olives

For the dressing

lemon, juiced
tbsp olive oil
salt and freshly ground black pepper

METHOD

1. Line four bowls with the lettuce leaves.
   Mix the sweetcorn with the peppers and
   cucumber, then divide between the bowls.

2. Top each one with half a boiled egg, a wedge
   of tomato and an olive.

3. Mix the lemon juice and oil with a pinch of
   salt and pepper.

4. Drizzle the dressing over the salads and
   serve immediately.

TOP TIP

Add a grated cheese of
your choice to add bulk
to this salad.

Courgette Soup

SERVES 4

PREPARATION TIME 15 MINUTES

COOKING TIME 30–40 MINUTES

INGREDIENTS

2 tbsp olive oil
1 onion, peeled and finely chopped
2 cloves garlic, finely chopped
1 kg / 2 ¼ lb / 4 ¼ cups courgettes
   (zucchinis), chopped
4 sprigs thyme
1 litre / 2 ¼ pints / 4 ¼ cups vegetable stock
½ lemon, juiced
60 ml / 2 oz / ¼ cup single (half-and-half) cream
salt and freshly ground black pepper

METHOD

1. Heat the oil in a large pan and sweat the onion until softened and translucent.

2. Add the garlic, courgettes and thyme, then cook very slowly over a low heat until the courgettes have darkened and are soft.

3. Add the stock and simmer for 20 minutes.

4. Blend two thirds of the soup with a stick blender, then return to the pan, reheat and season well. Add a splash of lemon juice.

5. Stir in the cream, season well, then heat gently and serve.

TOP TIP

Add a peeled, diced potato with the courgette, then mash when tender.

Strawberry and Mozzarella Salad

SERVES 4

PREPARATION TIME 5 MINUTES

INGREDIENTS

200 g / 7 oz / 2 cups strawberries, halved
200 g / 7 oz / 2 cups / 1 ⅓ cups mozzarella balls
a few sprigs of fresh thyme
1 tbsp extra virgin olive oil
sea salt and freshly ground black pepper

METHOD

1. Mix the strawberries with the mozzarella and thyme, then divide between four plates.

2. Dress with the olive oil and season well with sea salt and freshly ground black pepper.

TOP TIP

Replace the strawberries with halved cherry tomatoes.

Pumpkin Soup with Hazelnuts

SERVES 4

PREPARATION TIME 10 MINUTES

COOKING TIME 20 MINUTES

INGREDIENTS

1 onion, peeled and sliced
2 garlic cloves, sliced
30 g / 1 oz butter
1 large butternut squash or pumpkin, peeled, halved, deseeded and cut into chunks
2 sprigs thyme
1 litre / 2 ¼ pints / 4 ¼ cups vegetable stock
100 ml / 3 ½ fl. oz / ½ cup single (half-and-half) cream
100 ml / 3 ½ fl. oz / ½ cup hazelnuts (cobnuts), chopped
salt and freshly ground black pepper

METHOD

1. Sweat the onion and garlic in the butter in a large pan until golden and soft.

2. Add the squash and cook for five minutes, then add the thyme and stock.

3. Simmer for about 20 minutes or until the squash is tender.

4. Allow to cool a little, remove the thyme stems then blend in a food processor or with a stick blender until smooth.

5. Season and stir in the cream. Set aside.

6. Toast the hazelnuts under a hot grill for a few seconds only. Sprinkle on top of the hot soup and serve.

TOP TIP
Top with chopped chives for a herby kick.

Mains

Pumpkin and Butter Bean Stew

SERVES 4

PREPARATION TIME 20 MINUTES

COOKING TIME 5 HOURS

INGREDIENTS

tbsp olive oil

onion, finely chopped

cloves garlic, minced

50 g / 5 oz / 1 ½ cups small portobello mushrooms

00 g / 14 oz / 2 cups canned butter beans, drained and rinsed

pumpkin, peeled, deseeded and finely sliced

0 ml / 18 fl. oz / 2 cups vegetable stock

bay leaf

lt and freshly ground black pepper

nch of saffron strands

METHOD

1. Heat the olive oil in a casserole dish over a medium heat until hot.

2. Sweat the onion and garlic with a little salt for 6–7 minutes, stirring frequently, until softened.

3. Add the mushrooms, beans and pumpkin, then cover with the stock, stirring well. Add the bay leaf and pour into a slow cooker.

4. Cover and cook on a low setting for 5 hours.

5. Adjust the seasoning after 5 hours and ladle into a serving dish.

6. Garnish the dish with a few saffron strands before serving.

TOP TIP

Add a few chilli (chili) flakes to spice this dish to your own spice preference.

Stir-fried Vegetables

SERVES 4

PREPARATION TIME 2 MINUTES

COOKING TIME 6 MINUTES

INGREDIENTS

2 tbsp vegetable oil
2 cloves garlic, finely chopped
1 tbsp root ginger, finely chopped
1 fennel bulb, thinly sliced
½ Chinese cabbage, shredded
1 courgette (zucchini), diced
1 red pepper, julienned
2 tomatoes, cut into wedges
2 tbsp rice wine or dry sherry
1 tsp caster (superfine) sugar
1 tbsp light soy sauce

METHOD

1. Heat the oil in a large wok and fry the garlic and ginger for 30 seconds.

2. Add the vegetables and stir-fry for 4 minutes.

3. Mix the rice wine, sugar and soy together and add it to the wok.

4. Stir-fry until the vegetables are cooked through and evenly coated with the sauce. Serve immediately.

TOP TIP

Experiment with different vegetables to bulk out this stir-fry.

Paneer Jalfrezi

SERVES 4

PREPARATION TIME 10 MINUTES

COOKING TIME 4 HOURS 45 MINUTES

INGREDIENTS

- tbsp sunflower oil
- onions, chopped
- red pepper, deseeded and chopped
- green pepper, deseeded and chopped
- pinch of salt
- cloves garlic, minced
- cm (2 in) ginger, peeled and minced
- green chilli (chili), chopped
- tsp ground coriander seeds
- tsp ground cumin
- ½ tsp paprika
- ½ tsp garam masala
- tsp chilli (chili) powder
- tsp amchoor (dried mango powder)
- tsp sugar
- tomatoes, finely chopped
- 5 ml / 4 ½ fl. oz / ½ cup hot water
- 0 g / 10 ½ oz / 3 cups ready-made paneer cheese, cut into 2 cm (1 in) cubes

METHOD

1. Heat the oil in a large saucepan set over a medium heat.

2. Sauté the onion and peppers with a little salt for 4–5 minutes, stirring frequently.

3. Meanwhile, combine the garlic, ginger, chilli, spices, sugar, tomatoes, water and a little seasoning in a food processor. Pulse until smooth, then add to the onions and peppers.

4. Cook for a further 5 minutes, stirring occasionally. Add the paneer and stir well to coat in the sauce.

5. Pour into a slow cooker and cook on a low setting for 4 hours.

6. Adjust the seasoning to taste after 4 hours.

7. Spoon into serving bowls and serve immediately.

TOP TIP

Tinned tomatoes work equally well in this dish.

Asparagus Risotto

SERVES 4

PREPARATION TIME 10 MINUTES

COOKING TIME 25 MINUTES

INGREDIENTS

2 tbsp olive oil
40 g / 1 oz butter
1 onion, peeled and finely chopped
2 cloves garlic, minced
1 bunch asparagus, woody ends snapped off
320 g / 11 oz / 1 ⅓ cups risotto rice
100 ml / 3 ½ fl. oz / ½ cup dry white wine
1 litre / 2 ¼ pints / 4 ¼ cups vegetable stock
3 tbsp butter
120 g / 4 oz / ½ cup vegetarian Parmesan, grated
1 lemon, juiced and grated zest
salt and freshly ground black pepper

METHOD

1. Heat the oil and butter in a large pan and add the onion and garlic. Cook until soft and translucent.

2. Chop the asparagus into short lengths and add to the pan, then cook for a few minutes.

3. Add the rice and stir to coat in the butter. Pour in the wine and continually stir the rice while the wine is absorbed.

4. Once the wine has cooked in, reduce the heat and add the hot stock, a ladleful at a time, stirring continuously. This will give the risotto its creamy texture.

5. Keep stirring in the stock and tasting the rice. After about 15–20 minutes the rice should be soft but with a slight bite. If you've run out of stock before the rice is cooked, simply use water.

6. Season and remove from the heat. Add the butter and Parmesan and leave to melt into the risotto. Stir in the lemon zest and juice, then serve.

TOP TIP

Add a handful of peas to the risotto 5 minutes before the end of cooking.

Tofu and Vegetable Kebabs

SERVES 4

PREPARATION TIME 20 MINUTES

COOKING TIME 8 MINUTES

INGREDIENTS

1 tbsp dried herbes de Provence
1 tbsp olive oil
400 g / 14 oz / 2 ½ cups firm tofu, cubed
1 yellow pepper, cubed
1 large courgette (zucchini), quartered and sliced
8 cherry tomatoes

METHOD

1. Put 12 wooden skewers in a bowl of water and leave to soak for 20 minutes.

2. Meanwhile, stir the herbs into the oil and toss with the tofu and vegetables. Leave to marinate for 20 minutes.

3. Preheat the grill to its highest setting.

4. Thread the tofu and vegetables onto the skewers and spread them out on a large grill tray.

5. Grill the kebabs for 4 minutes on each side or until they are golden brown and cooked through.

TOP TIP
Replace the courgette (zucchini) with chunks of fresh pineapple.

Cajun Tofu Stew with Vegetables

SERVES 4

PREPARATION TIME 15 MINUTES

COOKING TIME 4 HOURS

INGREDIENTS

2 tbsp groundnut oil

2 large carrots, peeled and cubed

1 red pepper, deseeded and finely diced

2 sticks celery, sliced

300 g / 10 ½ oz / 2 cups tofu, cubed

110 g / 4 oz / 1 cup lumache pasta

400 g / 14 oz / 2 cups canned kidney beans,
    drained and rinsed

2 sheets dried wakame seaweed, cut into strips

250 ml / 9 fl. oz / 1 cup vegetable stock

2 tbsp dark soy sauce

2 tbsp flat-leaf parsley, finely chopped

4 sprigs of flat-leaf parsley

METHOD

1. Heat the groundnut oil in a large wok set over a moderate heat.

2. Sauté the carrots, pepper, celery and tofu for 3–4 minutes, stirring frequently. Spoon into a slow cooker and add the pasta, kidney beans, seaweed and stock.

3. Cover and cook on a medium setting for 4 hours.

4. Adjust the seasoning to taste with the soy sauce.

5. Spoon into serving bowls with a slotted spoon and garnish with a sprinkle of chopped parsley as well as a sprig of parsley leaves before serving.

TOP TIP

Replace the pasta with noodles and serve with the stock for a tasty soup.

Mushroom Gratin Dauphinoise

SERVES 4

PREPARATION TIME **15 MINUTES**

COOKING TIME **4 HOURS 10 MINUTES**

INGREDIENTS

85 g / 3 oz / 1 cup porcini mushrooms,
    brushed clean
250 ml / 9 fl. oz / 1 cup whole milk
250 ml / 9 fl. oz / 1 cup double (heavy) cream
pinch of ground nutmeg
55 g / 2 oz / ½ butter, softened
900 g / 2 lb / 6 cups maris piper potatoes, peeled
    and sliced thinly on a mandolin
85 g / 3 oz / 1 cup chanterelles, brushed clean
salt and freshly ground black pepper

METHOD

1. Combine the mushrooms, milk and double
   cream in a slow cooker with the nutmeg and
   some seasoning.

2. Cover and cook on a medium setting for
   3 hours until the mushrooms are soft.

3. Preheat the oven to 180°C (160°C fan) / 350F
   / gas 4.

4. Grease a baking dish with the butter and add
   a layer of potato slices.

5. Top with some of the mushrooms, then
   another layer of potato. Season in between
   layers, and repeat until all the mushrooms
   and potatoes are used up.

6. Pour the cooking liquor from the slow
   cooker into the dish and cover with foil.

7. Bake for 1 hour, then remove the foil and
   bake for a further 10 minutes to brown
   the top.

8. Remove from the oven and let it sit for
   10 minutes before serving.

TOP TIP

Serve with freshly
baked baguette for an
indulgent supper.

Cauliflower Gratin

SERVES 4–6

PREPARATION TIME 20 MINUTES

COOKING TIME 20 MINUTES

INGREDIENTS

1 head cauliflower
100 g / 3 ½ oz / ½ cup butter
2 tbsp plain (all-purpose) flour
1 tsp mustard powder
500 ml / 1 pint / 2 cups milk
2 bay leaves
grated nutmeg
¼ tsp mace
275 g / 10 oz / 1 ¼ cups Cheddar, grated

METHOD

1. Cut the cauliflower into florets and cook in boiling salted water for 5 minutes. Drain well and set aside.

2. Preheat the oven to 200°C (180°C fan) / 400F / gas 6.

3. Heat the butter in a pan and whisk in the flour and mustard powder to make a paste.

4. Gradually whisk in the milk and stir until thick and smooth. Add the bay leaves, nutmeg and mace and leave to simmer gently, stirring occasionally, for 10 minutes.

5. Stir in most of the cheese until melted.

6. Tip the cauliflower into a baking dish and spoon over the sauce. Sprinkle with the remaining cheese and bake for 20 minutes.

TOP TIP

Stir through 2 tbsp soy sauce just before serving.

Vegetable and Bean Stew

SERVES 4

PREPARATION TIME **15 MINUTES**

COOKING TIME **30 MINUTES**

INGREDIENTS

25 g / 1 oz butter
1 onion, peeled and finely sliced
2 carrots, peeled and finely sliced
2 leeks, white part only, finely sliced
100 g / 7 oz / ¾ cup button mushrooms, sliced
1 400 g can cannellini beans, drained
200 ml / 7 fl. oz / ¾ cup vegetable stock
2 tbsp dulse (sea lettuce), finely chopped
2 sprigs thyme
salt and freshly ground black pepper

METHOD

1. Heat the butter in a shallow pan and gently cook the onions without browning.

2. Add the carrots and leeks and cook until softened.

3. Add the mushrooms and cannellini beans, then pour in the stock.

4. Add the dulse and thyme and simmer very gently until the liquid has nearly evaporated and the vegetables are very tender.

5. Season and serve.

TOP TIP
Try using meatier butter beans instead of cannellini.

Spinach and Ricotta Cannelloni

SERVES 4

PREPARATION TIME 40 MINUTES

COOKING TIME 15 MINUTES

INGREDIENTS

12 cannelloni tubes or 12 sheets lasagne

For the filling
2 tbsp butter
olive oil
2 cloves garlic, chopped
1 kg / 2 lb / 4 ½ cups spinach leaves
¼ nutmeg, grated
400 g / 13 ½ oz / 1 ½ cups ricotta
2 tbsp vegetarian Parmesan, grated
salt and freshly ground black pepper

For the tomato sauce
2 tbsp olive oil
1 clove garlic, chopped
2 x 400 g can chopped tomatoes
½ bunch basil, chopped

METHOD

1. Preheat the oven to 180°C (160°C fan) / 350 / gas 5.

2. To make the filling, heat the butter in a larg pan with a little oil and cook the garlic for 2 minutes.

3. Add the spinach and nutmeg and stir until wilted.

4. Spoon into a sieve and press down firmly with a wooden spoon to extract as much liquid as possible. Once done, finely chop the spinach and leave to cool in a bowl.

5. Stir in the ricotta, Parmesan and seasonin

6. Spoon into the tubes or onto the lasagne sheets and roll up to make 12 cylinders, then lay in a greased baking dish.

7. To make the tomato sauce, heat the oil in a pan, then add the garlic and tomatoes. Leave to simmer, topped up with a little water, for 10 minutes, then add the basil.

8. Spoon over the cannelloni and bake for around 15 minutes until bubbling.

TOP TIP

Substitute the ricotta for mascarpone for a creamier sauce.

Savoury Vegetable Crumble

SERVES 8

PREPARATION TIME 5 MINUTES

COOKING TIME 40 MINUTES

INGREDIENTS

courgette (zucchini), chopped
aubergine (eggplant), chopped
spring onions (scallions), chopped
0 g / 3 ½ oz / ½ cup sun-dried tomatoes in oil,
  drained
g / 2 ½ oz / ⅓ cup butter
g / 1 ¾ oz / ⅓ cup plain (all-purpose) flour
g / 1 oz / ¼ cup ground almonds
g / 1 ½ oz / ½ cup feta, crumbled

METHOD

1. Preheat the oven to 180°C (160°C fan) / 350F / gas 4.

2. Mix together the courgette, aubergine, spring onions and sun-dried tomatoes and arrange them in a baking dish.

3. Rub the butter into the flour and stir in the ground almonds and feta, then season with salt and pepper.

4. Take a handful of topping and squeeze it into a clump, then crumble it over the vegetables.

5. Repeat with the rest of the crumble mixture, then press down into an even layer. Bake the crumble for 40 minutes or until the topping is golden brown.

TOP TIP
Add 1 large sweet potato, peeled and diced. This hearty vegetable adds subtle sweetness.

Stuffed Aubergines

SERVES 2

PREPARATION TIME 20 MINUTES

COOKING TIME 45 MINUTES

INGREDIENTS

2 aubergines (eggplants)
4 tbsp olive oil
1 onion, peeled and finely chopped
1 tsp dried oregano
2 cloves garlic
1 green pepper, finely chopped
1 yellow pepper, finely chopped
2 tomatoes, finely diced
bunch flat-leaf parsley, chopped
handful green olives, stoned
4 tbsp vegetarian Parmesan, grated
salt and freshly ground black pepper

METHOD

1. Preheat the oven to 200°C (180°C fan) / 400°F / gas 6.

2. Cut the aubergines in half lengthways, drizzle with 2 tbsp oil and bake in the oven for about 30 minutes until tender.

3. Remove the flesh with a spoon, leaving the skin intact and with a margin of flesh to support the structure.

4. Heat the remaining olive oil in the pan and cook the onion with oregano, garlic and peppers until softened.

5. Add the aubergine flesh and the rest of the ingredients and simmer for around 15 minutes.

6. Season and spoon into the aubergine skins, sprinkle over the Parmesan and put back into the oven until the cheese is bubbling. Serve immediately.

TOP TIP

Add mozzarella to the top and grill before serving.

Lemon Zest Risotto

SERVES 2

PREPARATION TIME 5 MINUTES

COOKING TIME 25 MINUTES

INGREDIENTS

1 litre / 1 pint 15 fl. oz / 4 cups vegetable stock
1 tbsp olive oil
1 onion, finely chopped
2 cloves garlic, crushed
1 lemon, zest finely pared
150 g / 5 ½ oz / ¾ cup risotto rice
100 g / 3 ½ oz / 1 cup asparagus spears, cut into short lengths
1 tbsp butter

METHOD

1. Heat the stock in a saucepan.

2. Heat the olive oil in a sauté pan and gently fry the onion for 5 minutes without browning.

3. Add the garlic and lemon zest and cook for 2 more minutes, then stir in the rice.

4. Add the asparagus, followed by two ladles of the hot stock.

5. Cook, stirring occasionally, until most of the stock has been absorbed, then add the next two ladles.

6. Continue in this way for around 15 minutes or until the rice is just tender.

7. Stir in the butter, then cover the pan and take off the heat to rest for 4 minutes.

8. Uncover the pan and season well with salt and pepper, then spoon into warm bowls.

TOP TIP

Replace the asparagus with mangetout and peas.

Italian-style Courgettes

SERVES 4

PREPARATION TIME 15 MINUTES

COOKING TIME 20 MINUTES

INGREDIENTS

4 courgettes (zucchinis)
extra virgin olive oil
200 g / 6 ½ oz / ¾ cup ricotta
1 tbsp parsley, finely chopped
1 tbsp basil, finely chopped
1 tbsp mint, finely chopped
4 tbsp vegetarian Parmesan, grated
salt and freshly ground black pepper

METHOD

1. Preheat the oven to 200°C (180°C fan) / 400 / gas 6.

2. Slice the courgettes in half lengthways and scoop out the flesh, leaving the sides intact

3. Finely dice the flesh. Heat 2 tbsp oil in a pa and cook the courgette flesh until tender. Tip into a bowl and leave to cool.

4. Once cool, stir into the ricotta and herbs, then season well.

5. Use a spoon to stuff the mixture into the courgettes, drizzle with oil and sprinkle ov the Parmesan.

6. Bake in the oven for about 20 minutes or until the courgettes are tender and bubbling

TOP TIP

Once cooked, sprinkle with toasted sunflower seeds for added crunch.

Chilli Con Carne

SERVES 2

PREPARATION TIME 20 MINUTES

COOKING TIME 4 HOURS

INGREDIENTS

tbsp vegetable oil
large onion, finely chopped
garlic cloves
red pepper, chopped
tsp hot chilli (chili) powder (or mild chilli
    powder if preferred)
tbsp paprika
tsp cumin
00 g / 1 lb vegetarian mince
½ tsp salt
50 ml / 5 fl. oz / ¾ cup water
2 tsp sugar
tsp oregano
x 400 g can tinned chopped tomatoes
tbsp tomato purée
vegetable stock cube
x 400 g red kidney beans cooked

METHOD

1. Pre-warm the slow cooker.

2. Heat the oil in a pan, then sauté the onions, garlic and pepper until soft. Add the chilli, paprika and cumin, stir well and cook for a further 4 minutes.

3. Add the vegetarian mince and brown thoroughly, then add the salt.

4. Pour over the water, sugar, oregano, tomatoes and purée. Crumble in the stock cube and stir thoroughly.

5. Transfer to the slow cooker. Cover and cook on a high setting for 3 ½ hours.

6. Drain the kidney beans and stir into the chilli con carne. Replace lid and cook for a further 30 minutes.

7. Serve immediately.

TOP TIP

Serve with tortilla chips, naan bread or cooked rice.

Ratatouille

SERVES 4

PREPARATION TIME 10 MINUTES

COOKING TIME 50 MINUTES

INGREDIENTS

4–6 tbsp olive oil
2 onions, peeled and finely sliced
2 aubergines (eggplants), cut in half lengthways
    and finely sliced
3 courgettes (zucchinis), cut in half lengthways
    and finely sliced
2 cloves garlic, finely chopped
3 red peppers, seeded and cut into strips
1 x 400g can chopped tomatoes
1 tsp coriander seeds, crushed
handful fresh basil leaves
salt and freshly ground black pepper

METHOD

1. Heat the oil in a pan and cook the onions
    until deep gold and sweet.

2. Add the aubergines and cook for 2 minutes,
    then add the courgettes and garlic. Cook for
    2 minutes, then add the peppers and cook
    for a further 5 minutes.

3. Add the tomatoes and coriander seeds and
    leave to simmer for at least 30 minutes over
    a very low heat, stirring occasionally, until
    the vegetables are very soft.

4. Season and sprinkle over the basil
    before serving.

TOP TIP

Cook for less time if you
want the vegetables to
have a crunchier
texture.

Leek, Tomato and Cheese Quiche

SERVES 6–8

PREPARATION TIME 5 MINUTES

COOKING TIME 40 MINUTES

INGREDIENTS

leeks, sliced
tbsp butter
large eggs, beaten
225 ml / 8 fl. oz / 1 cup double (heavy) cream
100 g / 3 ½ oz / ¾ cup cherry tomatoes, quartered
150 g / 5 ½ oz / 1 ½ cups Gruyère, grated
ready-made pastry case
salt and freshly ground black pepper

METHOD

1. Preheat the oven to 150°C (130°C fan) / 300F / gas 2.

2. Fry the leeks in the butter with a pinch of salt for 5 minutes or until starting to soften.

3. Whisk the eggs with the double cream until smoothly combined, then stir in the leeks, tomatoes and half of the Gruyère. Season with salt and pepper.

4. Pour the filling into the pastry case and scatter the rest of the cheese on top.

5. Bake for 35 minutes or until just set in the centre.

TOP TIP

Replace the cherry tomatoes with sun-dried tomatoes.

Red Pepper and Asparagus Paella

SERVES 4

PREPARATION TIME 5 MINUTES

COOKING TIME 30 MINUTES

INGREDIENTS

1 litre / 1 pint 15 fl. oz / 4 cups good quality
    vegetable stock
4 tbsp olive oil
1 onion, finely chopped
2 cloves of garlic, crushed
100 g / 3 ½ oz / 1 cup asparagus spears, cut into
    short lengths
1 courgette (zucchini), sliced
200 g / 7 oz / 1 cup paella rice
1 red pepper, sliced
2 tbsp flat-leaf parsley, chopped

METHOD

1. Heat the stock in a saucepan.

2. Heat the olive oil in a paella pan and gently
   fry the onion for 5 minutes without
   browning.

3. Add the garlic and cook for 2 more minutes
   then stir in the vegetables and rice and a
   little seasoning.

4. Stir well to coat with the oil, then pour in
   the stock and stir once more.

5. Arrange the pepper slices on top and bring
   to a simmer, then cook without stirring for
   10 minutes.

6. Cover the pan with foil or a lid, turn off the
   heat and leave to stand for 10 minutes.

7. Uncover the pan and sprinkle over the
   parsley before serving.

TOP TIP

Grill the pepper before adding to the paella, for a more intense taste.

Stir-fried Tofu with Vegetables

METHOD

1. Heat the oil in a large wok and fry the garlic and ginger for 30 seconds.

2. Add the tofu and stir-fry for 2 minutes. Add the baby corn and mangetout, then stir-fry for another 2 minutes.

3. Mix the cornflour with the rice wine, sugar and soy sauce and add it to the wok.

4. Stir-fry for 2 more minutes then serve immediately, garnished with the alfalfa sprouts on a bed of rice.

RVES 4

EPARATION TIME 5 MINUTES

OKING TIME 8 MINUTES

GREDIENTS

bsp vegetable oil
loves garlic, finely chopped
bsp root ginger, finely chopped
0 g / 7 oz / 1 ¼ cups firm tofu, cubed
g / 2 ½ oz / ¾ cup baby sweetcorn, halved lengthways
g / 2 ½ oz / ¾ cup mangetout
sp cornflour (cornstarch)
bsp rice wine or dry sherry
sp caster (superfine) sugar
bsp light soy sauce
g / 2 ½ oz / 1 ½ cups alfalfa sprouts
wn rice to serve

TOP TIP
Replace the cornflour (cornstarch) and rice wine with black bean sauce.

Vegetable and Pear Casserole

METHOD

1. Warm the slow cooker.

2. Blanch all the hard vegetables for 5 minutes, then drain and dry.

3. Heat the oil in a pan and gently sweat the onions, garlic and all the vegetables and pear pieces.

4. Add the vinegar, stock, tomato paste, herb and cider and bring to the boil for 5 minute

5. Place casserole into the slow cooker and cook on medium for 6 hours.

6. At the end of cooking, taste and add salt and black pepper as required.

7. Spoon into serving dishes and garnish with chopped parsley.

SERVES 4

PREPARATION TIME 25 MINUTES

COOKING TIME 6 HOURS

INGREDIENTS

2 tbsp sunflower or olive oil
1 medium onion, peeled and sliced in circles
1 garlic clove, crushed
2 carrots, roughly chopped and blanched for 5 minutes
1 celery stick, chopped
100 g / 4 oz / ¼ cup sweet potato sliced
100 g / 4 oz / ¼ cup salsify, peeled and sliced
100 g / 4 oz / ¼ cup shredded Savoy cabbage
100 g / 4 oz / ¼ cup cauliflower florets
1 tbsp tomato purée
4 beef tomatoes, skinned and sliced
3 tbsp cider vinegar
150 ml / 5 fl. oz / ½ cup dry cider
2 tbsp parsley, chopped
150 ml / 5 fl. oz / ½ cups vegetable stock
2 conference pears, cored and quartered
salt and freshly ground black pepper

TOP TIP

Add 1 tbsp of pear brandy to the casserole for a sweeter taste.

Sides and Snacks

Goats' Cheese Potato Cakes

SERVES 4

PREPARATION TIME 15 MINUTES

COOKING TIME 8 MINUTES

INGREDIENTS

300 g / 10 ½ oz / 2 cups leftover boiled potatoes, cold

1 egg yolk

Salt and freshly ground black pepper

100 g / 3 ½ oz / ⅔ cup fresh goats' cheese, cubed

1 tbsp fresh chives, chopped

1 tbsp flat-leaf parsley, chopped

50 g / 1 ¾ oz / ⅓ cup panko breadcrumbs

2 tbsp olive oil

serve

1 beefsteak tomato

30 g / 1 oz rocket leaves

A few sprigs parsley and chives

1 tbsp olive oil

METHOD

1. Mash the potato with the egg yolk and plenty of salt and pepper, then knead in the goats' cheese and herbs.

2. Divide the mixture into four and shape it into patties. Dip the potato cakes in the breadcrumbs to coat.

3. Heat the oil in a large frying pan and fry the potato cakes for 4 minutes on each side or until golden brown.

4. Meanwhile, cut four large slices from the middle of the tomato and cut the ends into cubes.

5. Put a tomato slice in the centre of each plate and arrange the rocket, cubed tomato and herbs round the outside.

6. Drizzle the salad with oil, then position a potato cake on top of each tomato slice.

TOP TIP

Serve with garden peas, topped with lemon juice and fresh mint.

Tofu and Carrot Broth

SERVES 4

PREPARATION TIME **10 MINUTES**

COOKING TIME **2 HOURS**

INGREDIENTS

2 tbsp groundnut oil
2 small onions, finely chopped
2 cloves garlic, minced
1 cm (½ in) piece of ginger, peeled and minced
4 medium carrots, peeled and diced
250 g / 9 oz / 2 cups tofu, cubed
550 ml / 1 pint / 2 ¼ cups vegetable stock
4 medium eggs, beaten
3 tbsp coriander (cilantro) leaves, finely chopped
salt and freshly ground black pepper

METHOD

1. Heat the groundnut oil in a large saucepan set over a medium heat until hot.

2. Sweat the onion, garlic, ginger and carrots for 7–8 minutes, stirring frequently until they start to soften. Add the tofu and stock, stirring well.

3. Pour into a slow cooker and cook for 2 hours on a medium setting.

4. Pour back into a saucepan after 2 hours and simmer over a medium heat.

5. Stir through the beaten egg and coriander until the egg starts to scramble and set.

6. Adjust the seasoning to taste, then pour into warm soup bowls before serving.

TOP TIP

Add a dash (½ tsp) of hot sauce at the end for a kick.

Sautéed Potatoes with Cumin and Thyme

RVES 4

EPARATION TIME 2 MINUTES

OKING TIME 18 MINUTES

INGREDIENTS

0 g / 1 lb 12 oz / 5 ⅓ cups Charlotte potatoes
bsp olive oil
sp ground cumin
bsp fresh thyme leaves
lt and freshly ground black pepper

METHOD

1. Boil the potatoes in salted water for 8 minutes, then drain well and leave to steam dry for 2 minutes.

2. Heat the oil in a large sauté pan.

3. Sprinkle the potatoes with cumin, thyme and plenty of salt and pepper then fry for 10 minutes, shaking the pan and stirring occasionally.

TOP TIP
Replace the cumin with thyme and fresh rosemary.

Vegetable Kebabs

SERVES 4

PREPARATION TIME 20 MINUTES

COOKING TIME 8 MINUTES

INGREDIENTS

1 tbsp dried herbes de Provence
3 tbsp olive oil
1 red pepper, cubed
1 green pepper, cubed
1 large courgette (zucchini), thickly sliced
½ aubergine (eggplant), cubed
100 g / 3 ½ oz / 1 ⅓ cups button mushrooms,
   thickly sliced
4 salad onions, halved

For the dip
1 tbsp lemon juice
½ tsp cracked black pepper
4 tbsp mayonnaise

METHOD

1. Put 12 wooden skewers in a bowl of water and leave to soak for 20 minutes.

2. Meanwhile, stir the herbs into the oil and toss with the vegetables. Leave to marinate for 20 minutes.

3. Make the dip by stirring the lemon juice and black pepper into the mayonnaise.

4. Preheat the grill to its highest setting.

5. Thread alternate vegetables onto the skewers and spread them out on a large grill tray.

6. Grill the kebabs for 4 minutes on each side or until they are golden brown and cooked through.

TOP TIP
Marinate cubed halloumi cheese with the vegetables.

Griddled Sweet Potato

SERVES 4

PREPARATION TIME 10 MINUTES

COOKING TIME 8–10 MINUTES

INGREDIENTS

large sweet potatoes, scrubbed
tbsp olive oil
inch dried chilli (chili) flakes (optional)
sprigs thyme leaves
salt and freshly ground black pepper

METHOD

1. Cut the potatoes across into thick rounds about 2 cm (¾ in) thick.

2. Rub with oil, chilli, thyme and seasoning, then score a cross-hatch into each side.

3. Heat a griddle pan or barbecue until very hot, then cook the potato slices until golden on both sides and tender all the way through; about 8–10 minutes per side. Turn them regularly to prevent burning.

TOP TIP
You can use this method with ordinary white potatoes as well.

Oven-baked Vegetables

METHOD

1. Preheat the oven to 200°C (180°C fan) / 400 / gas 6.

2. Mix all the vegetables with the thyme, garlic and olive oil and layer in a baking dish.

3. Season well with salt and pepper then bake for 45 minutes, stirring every 15 minutes.

SERVES 4

PREPARATION TIME 2 MINUTES

COOKING TIME 45 MINUTES

INGREDIENTS

4 baby artichokes, trimmed and halved
½ cauliflower, broken into florets
1 stick of celery, chopped
1 courgette (zucchini), cut into batons
8 mushrooms, sliced
4 tomatoes, cubed
2 tbsp fresh thyme leaves
2 cloves garlic, unpeeled and bruised
4 tbsp olive oil

TOP TIP
Any combination of vegetables will work well in this dish.

Aubergine alla Parmigiana

SERVES 4

PREPARATION TIME 15 MINUTES

COOKING TIME 45 MINUTES

INGREDIENTS

tbsp olive oil

tbsp dried oregano

aubergines (eggplants), thinly sliced lengthways

onion, peeled and chopped

cloves garlic, finely sliced

cinnamon stick

bunch basil

x 400 g can chopped tomatoes

balls mozzarella

0 g / 2 oz / ¼ cup vegetarian Parmesan, grated

METHOD

1. Preheat the oven to 200°C (180°C fan) / 400F / gas 6.

2. Pour the oil and oregano onto a baking sheet and coat the aubergine slices on both sides. Bake for 15 minutes or until tender and golden. Drain on kitchen paper.

3. Meanwhile, heat a little oil in a pan and gently fry the onion and garlic until completely soft.

4. Add the cinnamon stick, basil stalks and tomatoes and simmer for 20 minutes. Season well.

5. Spoon a little sauce into the bottom of a gratin dish, then layer aubergines, sauce and mozzarella to the top of the dish. Season to taste, finishing with a layer of sauce.

6. Sprinkle over the Parmesan and bake for 15–20 minutes until golden and bubbling.

TOP TIP
Add 2 thinly sliced courgettes (zucchinis), layering them with the aubergines.

Roasted Mushrooms with Garlic

SERVES 4

PREPARATION TIME 1 MINUTE

COOKING TIME 20 MINUTES

INGREDIENTS

4 large mushrooms
2 tbsp olive oil
25 g / 1 oz butter
4 cloves garlic, chopped
2 tbsp flat-leaf parsley, chopped

METHOD

1. Preheat the oven to 200°C (180°C fan) / 400F / gas 6.

2. Remove the stalks from the mushrooms and arrange cut side up in a baking dish.

3. Brush the mushrooms with oil and roast for 20 minutes.

4. Heat the butter in a small frying pan and cook the garlic until it just starts to turn golden, then quickly spoon the garlic butter over the mushrooms and sprinkle with parsley.

TOP TIP
Melt a cheese of your choice over the mushrooms in the last few minutes of cooking.

Confit Carrots

METHOD

1. Preheat oven to 140°C (120°C fan) / 275F / gas 1.

2. Lay the carrots in a baking dish and cover with oil, garlic and thyme, adding more oil if necessary to coat the carrots.

3. Bake in the oven for 2 hours until completely tender, then remove from the oven.

4. Fry the carrots briefly in a pan, then serve.

ERVES 4

REPARATION TIME 5 MINUTES

OOKING TIME 2 HOURS

NGREDIENTS

50 g / 12 oz / 1 ½ cups baby carrots, scrubbed
50 g / 9 oz / 1 cup olive oil
cloves garlic, finely sliced
sprigs thyme

TOP TIP
Add orange zest to the oil for a sweeter finish.

Creamy Mashed Potato

SERVES 4

PREPARATION TIME 2 MINUTES

COOKING TIME 15 MINUTES

INGREDIENTS

900 g / 2 lb / 6 cup potatoes, peeled and cubed
250 ml / 9 fl. oz / 1 cup whole milk
150 g / 5 ½ oz / ⅔ cup butter, cubed

METHOD

1. Put the potatoes in a pan of cold, salted water and bring to the boil.

2. Cook the potatoes for 10 minutes or until tender all the way through.

3. Tip the potatoes into a colander and leave to drain.

4. Put the saucepan back on the heat and add the milk and butter. Heat until the milk starts to simmer, then return the potatoes to the pan.

5. Take the pan off the heat and mash with a potato masher until smooth. Season to taste with salt and pepper and serve.

TOP TIP

For a hint of heat, stir in 1 tbsp wholegrain mustard.

Corn with Garlic and Parsley Butter

SERVES 4

PREPARATION TIME 20 MINUTES

COOKING TIME 16 MINUTES

INGREDIENTS

100 g / 3 ½ oz / ½ cup butter, softened
1 clove garlic, crushed
1 tbsp flat-leaf parsley, finely chopped
4 sweetcorn cobs
1 tsp salt

METHOD

1. Mix the butter with the garlic and parsley and season with salt and pepper. Shape into four small rounds and chill for 20 minutes.

2. Meanwhile, bring a large saucepan of water to the boil, add the salt and cook the sweetcorn for 8 minutes. Drain well.

3. Heat a griddle pan until smoking hot, then griddle the corn cobs for 8 minutes, turning occasionally.

4. Serve the corn on the cob with the butter rounds to coat.

TOP TIP
Add 1 finely chopped chilli (chili) to the garlic butter.

Desserts

Bread and Butter Pudding

ERVES 4–6

REPARATION TIME **15 MINUTES**

OOKING TIME **30–40 MINUTES**

NGREDIENTS

thick slices white bread, buttered
) g / 1 ¾ oz / ¼ cup sultanas, soaked in a
   little brandy
)0 ml / 10 fl. oz / 1 ¼ cups milk
) ml / 3 fl. oz / ¼ cup double (heavy) cream
) g / 1 ¾ oz / ¼ cup caster (superfine) sugar
eggs
reshly grated nutmeg

METHOD

1. Preheat the oven to 180°C (160°C fan) / 350F / gas 5 and butter the bottom and sides of a medium baking dish.

2. Cut each slice of bread into two triangles and arrange a layer in the base of the baking dish.

3. Sprinkle with the soaked sultanas, then add another layer of bread triangles over the top.

4. Whisk together the milk, cream, sugar and eggs until well combined, then pour over the bread layers.

5. Push the bread down to soak it thoroughly. The custard should just reach the top of the bread – if it doesn't, add a little more milk or cream. Grate over the nutmeg.

6. Bake in the oven for 30–40 minutes until set and golden.

TOP TIP

A couple of handfuls of dark chocolate chips add a luxurious twist.

Apple Crumble

SERVES 4

PREPARATION TIME 20 MINUTES

COOKING TIME 4 HOURS

INGREDIENTS

3 large Bramley apples (or any cooking apple)
½ lemon, juiced
2 tbsp golden syrup
125 g / 4 ½ oz / ½ cup butter
125 g / 4 ½ oz / ¾ cup plain (all-purpose) flour
60 g / 2 oz / ¼ cup rolled oats
125 g / 4 ½ oz / ⅔ cup, soft brown sugar

METHOD

1. Wash and peel the apples, core and cut into chunks.

2. Cover the apples with the lemon juice to prevent browning during the cooking process.

3. Place the apples at the bottom of your slow cooker and cover with the golden syrup.

4. Make the crumble by gently rubbing the butter and flour together until the mixture resembles breadcrumbs.

5. Add the oats and sugar to the mix.

6. Cover the apples with the crumble and mix evenly.

7. Cook on a low setting for 4 hours, then serve warm.

TOP TIP
Add ½ a cup of berries to the apples for a different taste and texture.

Crème Brûlée

METHOD

1. Preheat the oven to 180°C (160°C fan) / 350F / gas 5.

2. Tip the cream into a pan with the milk. Add the seeds from the vanilla pod and the pod itself. Heat almost to boiling point.

3. Whisk the egg yolks and sugar in a bowl until pale, then pour the hot cream into the egg yolks, whisking constantly. Strain through a sieve and stir well.

4. Sit four ramekins in a roasting tin and divide the mixture evenly between them. Pour in enough hot water to come halfway up the sides of the ramekins.

5. Bake for about 30 minutes, until set, then leave to cool on a wire rack and refrigerate until ready to serve.

6. Sprinkle over a thick layer of sugar and grill until deep golden and melted. Leave to cool and firm, then serve.

ERVES 4

REPARATION TIME **2 HOURS**

OOKING TIME **30 MINUTES**

NGREDIENTS

50 ml / 1 pint / 2 cups double (heavy) cream
00 ml / 3 ½ fl. oz / ½ cup milk
vanilla pod, halved
egg yolks
tbsp caster (superfine) sugar, plus extra
for the topping

TOP TIP
Serve with a few fresh raspberries or blueberries.

DESSERTS

Vanilla Millefeuille

SERVES 4

PREPARATION TIME 45 MINUTES

COOKING TIME 25–30 MINUTES

INGREDIENTS

1 sheet ready-made puff pastry
icing (confectioners') sugar

For the crème pâtissière

250 ml / 9 fl. oz / 1 cup full fat milk
½ vanilla pod, seeds removed
2 egg yolks
60 g / 2 oz / ¼ cup caster (superfine) sugar
2 tsp custard powder
1 tsp cornflour (cornstarch)
25 g / 1 oz butter

For the vanilla cream

50 ml / 1 ¾ oz / ¼ cup double (heavy)
    cream, whipped

METHOD

1. To make the crème pâtissière, bring the milk, vanilla pod and seeds to the boil in a heavy-bottomed pan.

2. In a bowl, whisk the egg yolks, sugar, custard powder and cornflour, then add a third of the milk to the bowl and whisk.

3. Remove the vanilla pod, bring the milk back to the boil and pour the egg mixture into the pan, whisking constantly until it re-boils.

4. Remove from the heat and whisk in the butter. Pour into a bowl and cover with cling film to prevent a skin forming, then set aside. Once cool, whisk until smooth, then fold in the whipped cream.

5. Preheat the oven to 190°C (170°C fan) / 375F / gas 5. Roll the pastry to 1.5 mm thick and prick with a fork all over.

6. Place on a lined baking sheet, then top with another layer of baking parchment and cover with a baking tray.

7. Bake in the oven according to packet instructions. Remove from the oven and increase the heat to 240°C (220°C fan) / 475F / gas 9.

8. Dust the smoothest side of the cooked pastry liberally with icing sugar and caramelize in the oven for a few seconds. Allow to cool, then cut into three equal strips.

9. When cold, pipe the vanilla cream onto one pastry strip. Top with a second layer, then pipe over more cream and top with the final pastry strip.

Chocolate Fondue

METHOD

1. Chop the chocolate and put it in a fondue bowl.

2. Bring the cream and brandy to simmering point, then pour it over the chocolate and stir until smooth.

3. Serve with the clementine segments and strawberries for dipping.

ERVES 4–6

REPARATION TIME **2 MINUTES**

OOKING TIME **4 MINUTES**

NGREDIENTS

00 g / 3 ½ oz / ¾ cup milk chocolate
50 ml / 3 ½ fl. oz / ⅔ cup double (heavy) cream
tbsp brandy
clementines, peeled
00 g / 7 oz / 1 cup strawberries, hulled
    and halved

TOP TIP

Replace the brandy with kirsch and stir 3 tbsp of sieved cherry jam (jelly) into the fondue.

Chocolate and Mint Mousse

SERVES 4

PREPARATION TIME 20 MINUTES

CHILLING TIME 6 HOURS

INGREDIENTS

200 g / 7 oz / ¾ cup dark chocolate
2 tbsp water
1–2 drops peppermint essence
4 eggs, separated
mint sprigs

METHOD

1. Melt the chocolate and water in a small bowl over a pan of simmering water.

2. Remove the melted chocolate from the heat and leave for 2 minutes.

3. Add the peppermint essence, then beat in the egg yolks. Leave to cool for 10 minutes or so.

4. Meanwhile whisk the egg whites to soft peaks. Fold into the chocolate mixture using a metal spoon.

5. Spoon into individual glasses or a bowl, cover with cling film and chill for at least 6 hours.

6. Decorate with mint sprigs and serve chilled.

TOP TIP

When melting the chocolate, make sure the bowl doesn't touch the water.

Baked Alaska

SERVES 4

PREPARATION TIME 20 MINUTES

COOKING TIME 5 MINUTES

INGREDIENTS

3 egg whites
a pinch of salt
1 tsp cream of tartar
200 g / 7 oz / ¾ cup caster (superfine) sugar
1 tsp vanilla extract
1 ready-made sponge base
1 kg / 2 lb / 4 cups ice cream, slightly softened

METHOD

1. Preheat the oven to its hottest temperature and place a shelf very low down.

2. Whisk the egg whites until foamy, then whisk in the salt and cream of tartar until it forms soft peaks.

3. Gradually whisk in the sugar a little at a time until thick and glossy, then fold in the vanilla extract.

4. Place the sponge base on a baking tray lined with greaseproof paper.

5. Using an ice cream scoop, place balls of ice cream on the base, leaving an edge around the outside.

6. Pile the meringue on top, spreading with a palette knife and ensuring the ice cream is completely covered.

7. Place under a grill for 2 minutes until golden. Serve immediately.

TOP TIP

Dip the ice cream scoop into hot water before scooping it out.

Poached Pears

SERVES 4

PREPARATION TIME **10 MINUTES**

COOKING TIME **45–50 MINUTES**

INGREDIENTS

4 pears, peeled, peelings reserved
500 ml / 1 pint / 2 cups white wine
2 tbsp runny honey
75 g / 2 ½ oz / ⅓ cup soft brown sugar
zest of ½ orange, plus the pared rind of the
    other half
1 cinnamon stick
1 vanilla pod, split
2 star anise

METHOD

1. Place the pear peelings and the rest of the poaching ingredients in a large pan and bring to the boil.

2. Simmer for 10 minutes to infuse.

3. Place the pears upright in the pan and poach gently for around 30 minutes or until completely tender.

4. Remove the pears from the liquor and set aside to cool.

5. Reduce the poaching liquor by half.

6. Serve the pears, with the poaching liquor spooned over.

TOP TIP
Drizzle some melted dark chocolate over the pears before serving.

Mississippi Mud Pie

ERVES 4

REPARATION TIME **1 HOUR**

OOKING TIME **40 MINUTES**

NGREDIENTS

5 g / 2 ½ oz / ⅓ cup butter, melted

00 g / 10 oz / 1 ¼ cups chocolate digestive
biscuits, crushed

or the filling

50 g / 5 oz / ⅔ cup dark chocolate, broken up

50 g / 5 oz / ⅔ cup butter, cubed

eggs

tbsp soft brown sugar

tbsp cocoa powder

tsp vanilla extract

nch cayenne pepper (optional)

50 ml / 5 fl. oz / ⅔ cup double (heavy)
cream, whipped

METHOD

1. Stir the crushed biscuits into the melted butter until thoroughly combined, then press into the base of a 23 cm (9 in) pie dish. Chill for 30 minutes.

2. Preheat the oven to 180°C (160°C fan) / 350F / gas 4.

3. Place the chocolate and butter in a bowl over a pan of simmering water, then stir until melted.

4. Remove from the heat and leave to cool for 5 minutes.

5. Whisk the eggs with the sugar until pale and tripled in volume.

6. Whisk in the melted chocolate in a steady trickle, then whisk in the cocoa powder, cream, vanilla and cayenne pepper if using.

7. Pour onto the biscuit base and bake for about 40 minutes until just firm. Leave to cool in the tin. It will sink slightly.

8. Serve with softly whipped cream.

TOP TIP

Serve with raspberries
to cut through
the chocolate.

Caramelized Spiced Mangoes

SERVES 4

PREPARATION TIME 5 MINUTES

COOKING TIME 15 MINUTES

INGREDIENTS

2 mangoes, peeled, stoned and cut into wedges
3 tbsp runny honey
2 tbsp dark rum
1 tbsp butter, melted
2 star anise

METHOD

1. Preheat the oven to 180°C (160°C fan) / 350F / gas 4.

2. Arrange the mango wedges in a small baking dish.

3. Mix the honey with the rum, melted butter and star anise and pour it over the top.

4. Bake in the oven for 15 minutes or until the mango is soft and starting to caramelize at the edges.

TOP TIP
Try other soft fruits in this dish, such as peaches.

Pineapple Tarte Tatin

SERVES 8

PREPARATION TIME **10 MINUTES**

COOKING TIME **25 MINUTES**

INGREDIENTS

2 tbsp butter, softened and cubed

3 tbsp dark brown sugar

400 g / 14 oz / 2 cups canned pineapple rings, drained

250 g / 9 oz all-butter puff pastry

METHOD

1. Preheat the oven to 220°C (200°C fan) / 425F / gas 7.

2. Dot the butter over the base of a large ovenproof frying pan and sprinkle over the sugar. Arrange the pineapple rings on top.

3. Roll out the pastry on a floured surface and cut out a circle the same size as the frying pan.

4. Lay the pastry over the pineapple and tuck in the edges. Transfer the pan to the oven and bake for 25 minutes or until the pastry is golden brown and cooked through.

5. Using oven gloves, put a large plate on top of the frying pan and turn them both over in one smooth movement to unmould the tart.

TOP TIP

Replace the pineapple with fresh or canned apricot halves.

Banoffee Pie

SERVES 6–8

PREPARATION TIME 2 HOURS

INGREDIENTS

400 g / 14 oz / 1 ½ cups digestive biscuits, crushed

200 g / 7 oz / ⅔ cup butter, melted

2 tins of condensed milk

2–3 ripe bananas

500 ml / 1 pint / 2 cups double (heavy) cream

1 tbsp dark chocolate, grated

METHOD

1. Combine the biscuits and butter in a bowl, then press into the bottom of a springform tin and refrigerate.

2. Cover the condensed milk tins completely in boiling water and boil for 2 hours. Make sure they are completely covered at all times, topping up if necessary.

3. Remove from the water and leave to cool. Open the tins and scoop out the toffee.

4. Blend the bananas with a spoonful of toffee in a food processor until smooth. Whisk the cream to soft peaks, then fold the banana mixture in until combined.

5. Spread half the banana cream over the biscuit base, then smooth over a layer of toffee, using a palette knife to even it out. Repeat, leaving a small amount of banana cream for piping.

6. Pipe rosettes of banana cream onto the top of the toffee, then decorate with grated chocolate. Refrigerate before serving.

TOP TIP

Try using shortbread instead of digestives for the base.

Passion Fruit and Lemon Cheesecake Pots

SERVES 4

PREPARATION TIME 40 MINUTES

INGREDIENTS

200 g / 7 oz / ¾ cup cream cheese
200 g / 7 oz / 1 cup condensed milk
2 lemons, juiced
1 tbsp poppy seeds
4 passion fruit, halved

METHOD

1. Beat the cream cheese with an electric whisk until smooth then whisk in the condensed milk.

2. Whisk in the lemon juice and poppy seeds until the mixture starts to thicken, then spoon into four glasses.

3. Leave to chill in the fridge for 30 minutes to firm up.

4. When the pots have set, spoon over the passion fruit pulp and seeds and serve.

TOP TIP
Replace the passion fruit with 3 finely chopped kiwi fruits.

DESSERTS

Mini Pavlovas with Fruit Coulis

SERVES 4

PREPARATION TIME 35 MINUTES

COOKING TIME 5 MINUTES

INGREDIENTS

250 g / 10 ½ oz / 1 ¼ cups mixed summer berries
2 tbsp caster (superfine) sugar
1 tbsp kirsch
250 ml / 9 fl. oz / 1 cup double (heavy) cream
4 meringue nests
mint leaves to garnish

METHOD

1. Reserve some of the berries for a garnish and put the rest in a saucepan with the sugar and kirsch.

2. Cook over a low heat for 5 minutes or until the berries start to burst.

3. Pour the mixture into a liquidizer and blend to a smooth sauce, then chill in the fridge for 25 minutes.

4. Whisk the cream until softly whipped and spoon it onto the meringue nests.

5. Arrange the mini pavlovas on a serving plate and drizzle the coulis over and around.

6. Scatter over the berries and garnish with mint leaves.

TOP TIP
Serve with whipped cream for a more decadent dessert.

Chocolate Samosas with Pineapple

SERVES 6

PREPARATION TIME 25 MINUTES

COOKING TIME 12–15 MINUTES

INGREDIENTS

225 g / 8 oz filo pastry

100 g / 3 ½ oz / ½ cup butter, melted

200 g / 7 oz / 2 cups dark chocolate (minimum 60% cocoa solids), finely chopped

1 pineapple, peeled and thinly sliced

METHOD

1. Preheat the oven to 180°C (160°C fan) / 350F / gas 4 and grease a large baking tray.

2. Cut the pile of filo sheets in half, then take one halved sheet and brush it with a little melted butter.

3. Arrange 1 tbsp of chopped chocolate at one end and fold the corner over, then triangle-fold it up.

4. Transfer the samosa to the baking tray and repeat with the rest of the filo and chocolate, then brush with any leftover butter.

5. Arrange the pineapple slices alongside the samosas and roast for 12–15 minutes or until the pastry is crisp and the pineapple is caramelized at the edges. Serve warm.

TOP TIP

Serve the pineapple with melted chocolate for an extra chocolate hit.

Apple Strudel

SERVES 4

PREPARATION TIME 30 MINUTES

COOKING TIME 35 MINUTES

INGREDIENTS

750 g / 1 ⅓ lb / 3 cups eating apples, peeled, cored and chopped
1 orange, juiced and zested
100 g / 3 ½ oz / ½ cup caster (superfine) sugar
¼ tsp ground cloves
2 tsp ground cinnamon
grated nutmeg
60 g / 2 oz / ¼ cup sultanas
6–8 sheets ready-made filo pastry
60 g / 2 oz / ¼ cup butter, melted
3 tbsp breadcrumbs

METHOD

1. Preheat the oven to 190°C (170°C fan) / 375F / gas 5.

2. Place the apples in a bowl and coat well with the orange juice to prevent browning. Add the zest, sugar, spices and sultanas, then mix well.

3. Brush each sheet of filo with melted butter, keeping the rest under a damp tea towel while not using.

4. Lay out a large piece of baking parchment and layer the sheets of filo on top of one another. Sprinkle the top sheet with breadcrumbs.

5. Spoon the apple mixture down the middle of the sheet.

6. Roll the pastry around the apple to make a fat sausage, using the parchment to help you roll.

7. Lift onto a baking tray, brush with more melted butter and bake for 35 minutes or until golden and crisp.

TOP TIP
Serve with warm custard or cold ice cream.

Lemon Meringue Pie

SERVES 6

PREPARATION TIME **15 MINUTES**

COOKING TIME **10 MINUTES**

INGREDIENTS

1 pastry case
1 jar lemon curd
4 large egg whites
110 g / 4 oz / ½ cup caster (superfine) sugar

METHOD

1. Preheat the oven to 200°C (180°C fan) / 400F / gas 6.

2. Fill the pastry case with lemon curd and smooth the top with a palette knife.

3. Whisk the egg whites until stiff, then gradually add the sugar and whisk until the mixture is thick and shiny.

4. Spoon the meringue on top of the lemon curd, making peaks with the spoon.

5. Bake for 10 minutes or until golden brown.

TOP TIP

The whisked egg whites should form soft peaks when ready.

Lemon Tart

SERVES *8*

PREPARATION TIME **5 MINUTES**

COOKING TIME **25–30 MINUTES**

INGREDIENTS

3 lemons, juiced
175 g / 6 oz / ¾ cup caster (superfine) sugar
2 tsp cornflour (cornstarch)
4 large eggs, beaten
225 ml / 8 fl. oz / ¾ cup double (heavy) cream
1 pastry case
lemon zest to garnish

METHOD

1. Preheat the oven to 170°C (150°C fan) / 340F / gas 3.

2. Stir the lemon juice into the caster sugar and cornflour to dissolve, then whisk in the eggs and cream.

3. Strain the mixture into the pastry case and bake for 25–30 minutes or until just set in the centre.

4. Garnish with lemon zest and serve either warm or at room temperature.

TOP TIP

Replace the lemons with the juice and zest from a large grapefruit.

Raspberry and Vanilla Trifle Pots

ERVES 6

REPARATION TIME 20 MINUTES

OOKING TIME 15–20 MINUTES

NGREDIENTS

00 g / 7 oz / 1 ¾ cup raspberries
small Madeira loaf cake

or the custard

vanilla pod, split lengthways
50 ml / 16 fl. oz / 1 ¾ cup whole (full-fat) milk
large egg yolks
5 g / 2 ½ oz / ½ cup caster (superfine) sugar
tsp cornflour (cornstarch)

METHOD

1. Scrape the seeds out of the vanilla pod and put them in a small saucepan with the milk. Bring to a simmer, then turn off the heat and leave to infuse for 5 minutes.

2. Whisk the egg yolks, sugar and cornflour together, then gradually whisk in the milk.

3. Scrape the mixture back into the saucepan, then cook over a medium heat until the mixture thickens, stirring constantly. Remove from the heat and plunge the base of the pan into cold water.

4. Mash a third of the raspberries with a fork, then stir in the rest of the whole raspberries.

5. Put a spoonful of the raspberry mixture in the bottom of six glasses and crumble over half of the cake.

6. Top with half the custard, then add half of the remaining raspberries. Top with the rest of the cake, then the rest of the custard and finish each glass with a ring of raspberries.

TOP TIP
Replace the raspberries with strawberries.

195

Quick Chocolate Mousse

SERVES 4

PREPARATION TIME 30–40 MINUTES

INGREDIENTS

200 g / 7 fl. oz / ¾ cup double (heavy) cream
200 g / 7 oz / 2 cups milk chocolate, chopped
2 egg whites
4 tbsp caster (superfine) sugar
chocolate sugar balls, to decorate

METHOD

1. Heat the cream to simmering point, then pour it over the chocolate and stir until smooth. Leave to cool for 10 minutes.

2. Whip the egg whites until stiff, then whisk in the sugar.

3. Stir a spoonful of the egg white into the cooled chocolate mixture, then fold in the rest with a big metal spoon. Make sure to keep as many of the air bubbles as intact as possible.

4. Spoon the mousse into four glasses and chill for 20 minutes.

5. Decorate with chocolate sugar balls before serving.

TOP TIP

Replace the milk chocolate with white chocolate and add orange zest.

Bakes and Cakes

Parsley and Feta Loaf Cake

SERVES 8

PREPARATION TIME **10 MINUTES**

COOKING TIME **55 MINUTES**

INGREDIENTS

300 g / 10 ½ oz / 2 cups self-raising flour
2 tsp baking powder
250 g / 9 oz / 1 ¼ cup butter, softened
5 large eggs
150 g / 5 oz feta, cubed
3 tbsp flat-leaf parsley, chopped

METHOD

1. Preheat the oven to 170°C (150°C fan) / 340F / gas 3 and line a large loaf tin with non-stick baking paper.

2. Sieve the flour and baking powder into a mixing bowl and add the butter and eggs.

3. Beat the mixture for 4 minutes or until smooth and well whipped.

4. Fold in the feta and parsley, then scrape the mixture into the loaf tin.

5. Bake for 55 minutes or until a skewer inserted in the centre comes out clean.

6. Transfer the cake to a wire rack and leave to cool completely before serving.

TOP TIP
Replace the parsley with chopped fresh dill.

Sesame and Poppy Seed Focaccia

SERVES 6

PREPARATION TIME 2 HOURS 30 MINUTES

COOKING TIME 25–35 MINUTES

INGREDIENTS

300 g / 10 ½ oz / 2 cups strong white bread flour
½ tsp easy-bake dried yeast
1 tsp fine sea salt
2 tbsp olive oil

To finish
50 ml / 1 ¾ fl. oz / ¼ cup olive oil
50 ml / 1 ¾ fl. oz / ¼ cup warm water
½ tsp fine sea salt
1 tbsp sesame seeds
1 tbsp poppy seeds

METHOD

1. Mix together the flour, yeast and salt, then stir in the oil and 300 ml / 10 fl. oz / 1 ¼ cups of warm water.

2. Knead the mixture on a lightly oiled surface for 10 minutes or until smooth and elastic. Leave the dough to rest, covered with oiled cling film, for 1–2 hours or until doubled in size.

3. Oil a rectangular cake tin, then stretch out the dough to cover the base.

4. Cover the focaccia with oiled cling film and leave to prove for 1 hour or until doubled in size.

5. Preheat the oven to 220°C (200°C fan) / 430F / gas 7.

6. Put the oil, water and salt in a jar and shake well. Pour it all over the dough, then sprinkle with the seeds.

7. Bake for 25–35 minutes or until the top is golden and the base is cooked through.

8. Leave to cool on a wire rack before cutting into squares.

TOP TIP

Replace the poppy seeds with black onion seeds for a different taste.

Olive and Rosemary Mini Muffins

MAKES 24

PREPARATION TIME 15 MINUTES

COOKING TIME 10–15 MINUTES

INGREDIENTS

2 large eggs
120 ml / 4 fl. oz / ½ cup sunflower oil
180 ml / 6 fl. oz / ⅔ cup Greek yogurt
2 tbsp vegetarian Parmesan, finely grated
225 g / 8 oz / 1 ½ cup plain (all-purpose) flour
2 tsp baking powder
½ tsp bicarbonate of (baking) soda
½ tsp salt
75 g / 2 ½ oz / ½ cup black olives, stoned
    and chopped
2 tbsp fresh rosemary, chopped

METHOD

1. Preheat the oven to 180°C (160°C fan) / 350F / gas 4 and line a 24-hole mini muffin tin with paper cases.

2. Beat the egg in a jug with the oil, yogurt and cheese until well mixed.

3. Mix the flour, raising agents, salt, olives and rosemary in a bowl, then pour in the egg mixture and stir to combine.

4. Divide the mixture between the paper cases, then bake in the oven for 10–15 minutes.

5. Test with a wooden toothpick, if it comes out clean, the muffins are done.

TOP TIP

Replace the olives with goats' cheese, cut into cubes.

Parmesan, Thyme and Peppercorn Cookies

MAKES **36**

PREPARATION TIME **15 MINUTES**

COOKING TIME **10–15 MINUTES**

INGREDIENTS

2 large eggs
110 ml / 4 fl. oz / ½ cup sunflower oil
110 ml / 4 fl. oz / ⅔ cup Greek yogurt
110 g / 4 oz / 1 cup vegetarian Parmesan, grated
225 g / 8 oz / 1 ½ cup plain (all-purpose) flour
2 tsp baking powder
½ tsp bicarbonate of (baking) soda
½ tsp salt
2 tbsp fresh thyme leaves
1 tbsp pink peppercorns, crushed

METHOD

1. Preheat the oven to 180°C (160°C fan) / 355F / gas 4 and line two baking trays with greaseproof paper.

2. Beat the eggs in a jug with the oil, yogurt and Parmesan until well mixed.

3. Mix the flour, raising agents, salt, thyme and peppercorns in a bowl, then pour in the egg mixture.

4. Stir everything just enough to combine.

5. Drop heaped teaspoons of the mixture spaced out on the baking trays and bake in batches for 10–15 minutes or until golden brown.

6. Transfer to a wire rack and leave to cool.

TOP TIP
Replace the thyme with 2 tbsp of chopped fresh rosemary.

Pretzels

MAKES 4

PREPARATION TIME 2 HOURS 30 MINUTES

COOKING TIME 10 MINUTES

INGREDIENTS

300 g / 10 ½ oz / 2 cups strong white bread flour
½ tsp easy-bake dried yeast
1 tbsp butter, melted
1 tsp salt
1 egg, beaten
1 tbsp sugar nibs

METHOD

1. Mix the flour, yeast, butter and salt together in a bowl and stir in 200 ml / 6 ¾ fl. oz / 1 cup of warm water.

2. Bring the mixture into a dough with your hands and knead for 10 minutes.

3. Leave to rest in a warm place for 1 hour or until doubled in size.

4. Divide the dough into four even pieces and roll each one into a long sausage.

5. Twist into a classic pretzel shape and transfer to an oiled baking tray.

6. Prove for 45 minutes in a warm place.

7. Preheat the oven to 220°C (200°C fan) / 425F / gas 7.

8. When the pretzels are well risen, brush them with egg and sprinkle with sugar nibs, then bake for 10 minutes or until golden brown and cooked through.

TOP TIP

Try other shapes if you are struggling with the classic pretzel shape.

Lemon Drizzle Cake

SERVES 6

PREPARATION TIME 25 MINUTES

COOKING TIME 40–45 MINUTES

INGREDIENTS

120 g / 4 oz / ½ cup butter, softened
175 g / 6 oz / ¾ cup caster (superfine) sugar
2 eggs
1 lemon, grated zest
175 g / 6 oz / ¾ cup self-raising flour
100 ml / 3 ½ fl. oz / ½ cup milk

For the syrup
2 lemons, juiced
100 g / 3 ½ oz / ½ cup icing (confectioners') sugar

For the glaze
½ lemon, juiced
150 g / 5 oz / ⅔ cup icing (confectioners') sugar

METHOD

1. Preheat the oven to 180°C / 350F / gas 4. Grease and line a loaf tin.

2. Cream the butter and sugar until pale and creamy, then whisk in the eggs a little at a time.

3. Whisk in the zest, then, using a metal spoon, fold in the flour and salt and stir in the milk.

4. Spoon into the loaf tin and bake for 40–45 minutes until a skewer inserted into the centre comes out clean. Set aside.

5. Heat the lemon juice and sugar in a pan until the sugar dissolves. Puncture the surface of the cake with a skewer and pour over the hot syrup. Leave to cool completely, then remove from the tin.

6. Whisk together the lemon juice and sugar to make the glaze, then drizzle over the top of the cake.

TOP TIP
Make more icing to coat the top of the cake, then decorate with lemon slices.

Millionaire's Shortbread

MAKES 9

PREPARATION TIME **20 MINUTES**

COOKING TIME **3 HOURS 15–20 MINUTES**

INGREDIENTS

230 g / 8 oz / 1 ½ cups plain (all-purpose) flour

2 tbsp cocoa powder

75 g / 2 ½ oz / ⅓ cup caster (superfine) sugar

150 g / 5 oz / ⅔ cup butter, cubed

50 g / 1 ¾ oz / ¼ cup granulated sugar

For the topping

1 can condensed milk

200 g / 7 oz milk chocolate

METHOD

1. To make the caramel layer in advance, put the unopened can of condensed milk in a saucepan of water and simmer for 3 hours, adding more water as necessary. Make sure it doesn't boil dry. Leave the can to cool.

2. Preheat the oven to 180°C (160°C fan) / 355F / gas 4 and line a 20 cm (8 in) square cake tin with greaseproof paper.

3. Mix together the flour, cocoa and sugar in a bowl, then rub in the butter. Knead gently until the mixture forms a smooth dough, then press it into the bottom of the tin in an even layer.

4. Bake the shortbread for 15–20 minutes, turning the tray round halfway through. Leave to cool.

5. Open the can of condensed milk and beat until smooth. Spread it over the shortbread and chill for 1 hour.

6. Melt the chocolate in a microwave or bain-marie and spread it over the caramel.

7. Chill in the fridge for 30 minutes.

TOP TIP

Garnish the tops of the shortbread with a pinch of flaked sea salt.

213

Carrot Cake

SERVES 4

PREPARATION TIME 20 MINUTES

COOKING TIME 1 HOUR 30 MINUTES

INGREDIENTS

300 g / 10 oz / 1 ¼ cups plain (all-purpose) flour
1 tsp ground cinnamon
1 tsp baking powder
½ tsp bicarbonate of (baking) soda
200 g / 7 oz / ¾ cup soft dark brown sugar
4 eggs
250 ml / 9 fl. oz / 1 cup vegetable oil
2 oranges, zested
200 g / 7 oz / ¾ cup carrots, peeled and grated
125 g / 4 oz / ½ cup butter, softened
2 tbsp icing (confectioners') sugar
250 g / 9 oz / 1 cup cream cheese
½ lemon, zested

METHOD

1. Preheat the oven to 150°C (130°C fan) / 300F / gas 2. Grease and line a 20 cm (8 in) square cake tin.

2. Sieve the flour into a bowl with cinnamon, baking powder and bicarbonate of soda, then stir in the sugar.

3. Beat the eggs with the oil and fold into the flour with the carrots and orange zest.

4. Spoon into the cake tin and bake for about 1 ½ hours until a skewer inserted into the centre comes out clean. Leave to cool.

5. Beat the butter and sugar together until pale, then beat in the cream cheese and lemon zest. Chill until spreadable and cover the cake using a palette knife to smooth.

TOP TIP

A pinch of mixed spice with the cinnamon will add a touch of warmth.

Gingerbread Cake

SERVES 6

PREPARATION TIME 20 MINUTES

COOKING TIME 45 MINUTES

INGREDIENTS

250 g / 9 oz / 1 cup self-raising flour
1 tsp baking powder
½ tsp bicarbonate of (baking) soda
½ tsp ground ginger
½ tsp mixed spice
75 g / 2 ½ oz / ⅓ cup caster (superfine) sugar
75 g / 2 ½ oz / ⅓ cup unsalted butter, melted
200 ml / 7 fl. oz / ¾ cup milk
1 egg
2–3 tbsp stem ginger, finely chopped

METHOD

1. Preheat the oven to 200°C (180°C fan) / 400F / gas 6. Grease and line a loaf tin.

2. Combine the dry ingredients in a bowl.

3. Pour the milk into a measuring jug and crack in the egg, then whisk with a fork.

4. Pour the liquid ingredients into the dry ingredients, stirring with a wooden spoon. The batter should remain lumpy – do not whisk until smooth. Add the stem ginger to the batter and stir in.

5. Pour into the loaf tin and bake in the oven for about 45 minutes or until a skewer inserted into the centre comes out clean.

6. Remove to a wire rack and allow to cool.

TOP TIP
Add a handful of chopped mixed nuts to the batter for extra crunch.

Orange Loaf Cake

SERVES 8

PREPARATION TIME 20 MINUTES

COOKING TIME 50–60 MINUTES

INGREDIENTS

120 g / 4 oz / ½ cup butter, softened

250 g / 9 oz / 1 cup caster (superfine) sugar

3 eggs, beaten

1 orange, juiced and zested

250 g / 9 oz / 1 cup plain (all-purpose) flour

1 tsp baking powder

1 orange, juiced

3–4 tbsp honey

2 drops orange blossom water (optional)

To decorate

1 orange, sliced into rounds and baked on a rack
at 120°C / 250F for 2 hours

METHOD

1. Preheat the oven to 180°C (160°C fan) /
   350F / gas 5. Grease and line a loaf tin.

2. Cream the butter and sugar together until
   pale and creamy, then add the beaten eggs
   a little at a time, beating thoroughly after
   each addition.

3. Fold in the zest and juice, flour and baking
   powder. Pour into the loaf tin.

4. Bake for 50–60 minutes or until an inserted
   skewer comes out clean. Turn out of the tin
   onto a wire rack.

5. Meanwhile heat the juice and honey, then
   add the orange blossom water if using.
   Pierce the cake with a skewer a few times
   and drizzle the syrup over and leave to
   soak in.

6. Decorate with the dried orange slices.

TOP TIP

Stir orange juice and
zest into mascarpone
and serve alongside.

INDEX